Contents

TRAINING YOUR
PET HAMSTER

Gerry Bucsis and
Barbara Somerville

With photographs by the authors

BARRON'S

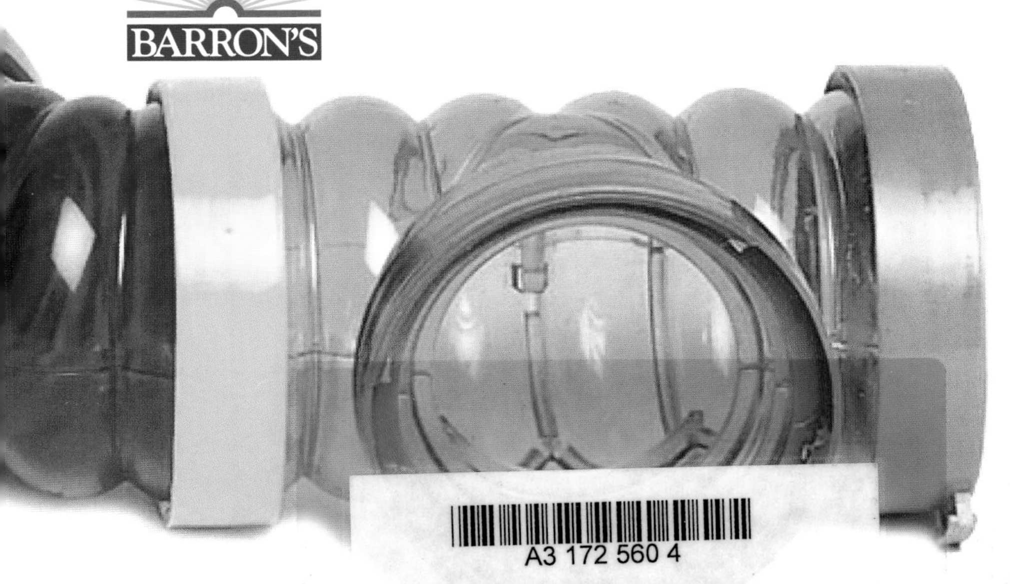

Acknowledgments

Special thanks to

• Our families for their support, understanding, and encouragement.

• Our editor, Anna Damaskos—for her great sense of humor and no-nonsense advice.

• Our friends: Amanda and her hamster, Pancake; Elise and her hamster, Figment; Kayla and her hamster, Mr. Jingles; Paige and Taylor and their hamster, Fudgee-o; Wendy and her hamster, Speedy—for letting their pets be photographed. What fun we had!

• Jason Casto for all of his help and support.

• Steve, of Steve's Wonderful World of Pets, for all the fun Pet Days.

• The following companies for their help and cooperation: Absorption Corporation; Eight In One Pet Products, Inc.; Essex Topcrop Sales, Ltd.; Evsco Pharmaceuticals; Kaytee Products, Inc.; Penn-Plax S.A.M.; Rolf C. Hagen, Inc.; SunSeed Company, Inc.; "Super Pet" Pets International, Ltd.; Vitakraft.

All inquiries should be addressed to:

Barron's Educational Series, Inc.

250 Wireless Boulevard

Hauppauge, New York 11788

http://www.barronseduc.com

International Standard Book No. 0-7641-2013-1

Library of Congress Catalog Card No. 2002018505

Library of Congress Cataloging-in-Publication Data

Bucsis, Gerry.

Training your pet hamster / by Gerry Bucsis and Barbara Somerville.

p. cm.

Includes bibliographical references and index.

ISBN 0-7641-2013-1

1. Hamstsers as pets—Training. I. Somerville, Barbara. II. Title.

SF459.H3 B83 2002

636.9′356—dc21 2002018505

Printed in China

987

Photo Credits

Photos on pages 4, 5, 6, 34, 39, 46–47 [lower photo], 67, and 69 are courtesy of Rolf C. Hagen, Inc.

Photos on pages 2, 3, 17 [lower photo], 18, 25, 38, 41, 43, 48 [upper photo], 65 [upper photo], inside front cover are courtesy of "Super Pet" Pets International, Ltd.

Product Information

Yogies, pg. 11 is courtesy of Eight In One Pet Products, Inc.

Nutra-Puffs, pg. viii; Yogurt Chips, pg. 29; Wild Berry Treat stick, pg. 68; and Mini-pop, pg. 73 are courtesy of Kaytee Products, Inc.

Wooden bridge, pg. 8; hamster grass, pg. 12; Small Pals Pen, pg. 22; wheel, pg. 44; hamster harness and leash, pg. 60; clear Rock & Roll Hamster Ball, pgs. 62 and 63; wooden bird ladder, pg. 68 are courtesy of Rolf C. Hagen, Inc.

Swing O'Fun, pg. 49 and Toob-A-Brush, pg. 80 are courtesy of Penn-Plax S.A.M.

Healthy Hearts, pg. 84 is courtesy of SunSeed Company, Inc.

Sleep houses, pgs. 9 and 33; Critter Ka-Bobs and Salt Savors, pg. 13; Bark Bites, pgs. 13 and 32; dishes, front cover and pgs. 14 and 83; Hamster Bites, pgs. 16, 36, and 85; Puzzle Playground, pgs. 19, 47, 70, and 76; Loop-D-Loop, pg. 21; Swiss Chews, pg. 37; Critter Trail Outhouse, pg. 42; wheels, pg. 45; Roll-a-nest toys, pg. 48; Woodkins', pgs. 49 and 72; CritterTrail cage, inside back cover and pg. 57; Critter Cruiser, pg. 62; blue Run-about Ball, pg. 63; bamboo ball, pg. 65; CritterTrail Fun Forms, pg. 66; Sleep Sack, pg. 72; Carnival of Crinkles, pg. 74; Critter Cubby Hole drum, pg. 75; and Safety Ramps, pg. 81 are courtesy of "Super Pet" Pets International, Ltd.

Small Animal Waffles, pg. 8 and Small Animal Cake, pg. 12 are courtesy of Vitakraft.

Important Note

This book deals with the keeping and training of pet hamsters. In working with these animals, you may occasionally sustain scratches or bites. Administer first aid immediately, and seek medical attention if necessary. There are a few diseases of domestic hamsters that can be transmitted to humans, and some people are allergic to hamster hair, dander, saliva, urine, and/or feces. If you are at all concerned that your own health, or the health of a family member, might be affected by contact with hamsters, consult with your doctor *before* bringing one home. Some people have compromised immune systems and should not be exposed to animals. If in doubt, check with your physician.

Children should be taught how to handle hamsters safely. Never leave small children or pets alone with a hamster. To prevent electric accidents, make sure that your hamster cannot gnaw on electric cords.

If your hamster shows *any* sign of illness, take it to a veterinarian immediately. Delay could be fatal for your pet.

The authors and the publisher assume no responsibility for and make no warranty with respect to results that may be obtained from procedures cited. Neither the authors nor the publisher shall be liable for any damage resulting from reliance on any information contained herein, whether with respect to procedures, or by reason of any misstatement, error, or omission, negligent or otherwise, contained in this work. Information contained herein is presented as a reference only.

Introduction

Rats, mice, gerbils, guinea pigs—these days, small animals are really coming into their own as pet possibilities. And which pet is right at the top of the small-animal popularity polls? You've got it . . . the hamster. This comes as no surprise. You just have to look at a cage full of hamster hopefuls to understand their instant appeal. They're cute, they're fluffy, they have big eyes and pouches to match. Best of all, these round little balls of fur are virtually tailless, a major selling point for many people who are turned off by long rodent tails.

But hamsters have a lot more going for them than their good looks. To start with, they're cheap to buy and inexpensive to maintain. Being small, they fit into any house, room, dorm, or apartment. And, being quiet, they never annoy the neighbors (unless, of course, that running wheel *squeaks*, *squeaks*, *squeaks*!). As an added bonus, these minimammals make ideal pets for today's busy families. Are you out all day at school or at work? No need for a guilt trip—hamsters sleep all day anyway. They don't get up until the late afternoon or evening, just when the family is on hand to play with them. Is there not much time in your busy schedule for bathing and grooming a pet? Don't worry, hamsters are self-groomers, and they don't need baths. Even better, they don't need to be taken out for walks in all types of weather . . . a huge plus for time-strapped owners.

So much for the positive reasons for making a hamster part of your family. Now, are there any negatives? The answer, of course, is "yes." There are drawbacks to every pet, and the hamster is no exception. For example, hamsters can't have their sleep disturbed or they'll get sick. So, when it comes to playtime, you have to go by your hamster's timetable, not yours. And although hamsters look cuddly, most are not buddy-buddy by nature—they have to learn to love the humans in their lives.

This is where *Training Your Pet Hamster* comes in. In this user-friendly book, you'll learn how and when to pick the right hamster pupil and how to train that pupil to become a first-rate people pet. Along the way you'll learn specific techniques for teaching your pet positive behaviors like coming on cue, potty training, and walking on a leash. You'll also learn how to deal

Is a hamster the right pet for you?

with negative behaviors such as your minimuncher's destructive gnawing. Then there are the fun chapters that teach you ways to make the most of pet playtime.

Many hamster owners don't understand their pet's needs, and as a result, their hamsters are left to languish in tiny cages without stimulation. Don't let this happen to your pet! Instead, follow the advice given in *Training Your Pet Hamster* so that your little critter can have the best-possible quality of life. After all, isn't that what responsible pet ownership is all about?

Chapter One

Pre-Pet Preparations

Before you buy

You might think that a hamster would be the ideal pet for your household, but are you sure? Do you know the care requirements for hamsters? Do you know anything about their behavior? Do you know how long they live? Do you know anything about the different types of hamster? Do you have a realistic idea of the time commitment involved?

When it comes to buying a pet, impulse buying is out and research is in. Make it your business to find out the hamster facts. Read books, surf the Internet, visit pet shops, talk to hamster owners—*then* decide if you're still eager and able to give a hamster a happy home. You are? Now, be a responsible owner and get everything ready at home *before* purchasing your pet. First on the list is the cage.

A happy home

The big myth about hamster homes is that a small cage suits a small hamster. Forget this myth. The fact of the matter is that hamsters need as extensive a cage setup as possible. Why? In their natural desert habitat, hamsters range far and wide every night foraging for food—they can cover miles at a time. So, in captivity, they do best in a cage layout that lets them mimic their natural behavior. Buy your pet a home that gives him room to roam, room to stash food, room for separate sleeping quarters, and room for toilet duties.

If you try to keep your hamster in a 12-inch × 12-inch × 12-inch (30-cm × 30-cm × 30-cm) cube, he won't be happy. In fact, he's likely to get bored and stressed from inactivity. Prolonged stress can lead to health problems and a shorter life span. Constant boredom can lead to behavior problems such as biting and obsessive/compulsive behavior. A cooped-up hamster will often gnaw at the cage bars, claw at the walls, and run back and forth endlessly. Avoid these problems by picking out a habitat that gives your pet plenty of room for running around.

An extensive cage setup gives your hamster the roam room he needs.

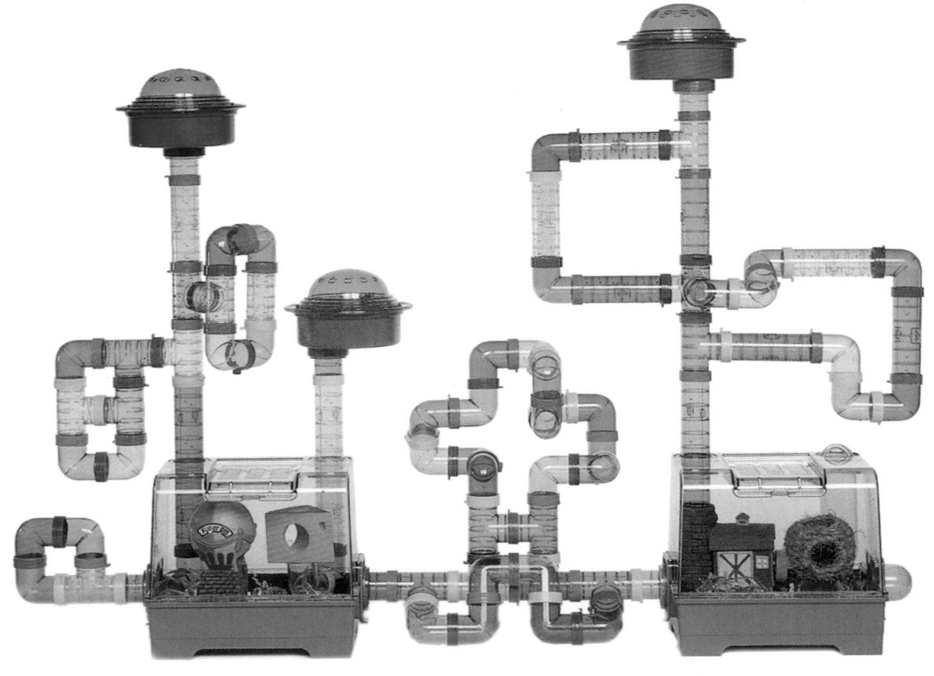

If you can't afford a large enough cage setup right now, please postpone your hamster purchase until you can afford something suitably spacious. It's better to save up and buy the right cage than to make your hamster suffer in the wrong cage. After all, you want to give your pet the best-possible quality of life.

Hamster habitats

Hamster habitats are modular units made specifically to house hamsters. They're widely available wherever hamster products are sold. The great thing about these habitats is that you can mix and match the different units and connecting tubes to make as large a layout as you can afford or find space for—the combinations are endless.

And it's a combination you'll need, as one module is not big enough for a hamster. Think of two as the minimum, and add more as your budget allows. What's nice about these hamster homes is that the units come in different materials that can be mixed and matched for your hamster's year-round comfort. Try combining a plastic cage module with a wire garden gazebo—the plastic cage will be toasty in the winter, and the wire one will let in the air during the summer.

The biggest plus with these made-for-hamster homes is that they've been designed to mimic a hamster's natural habitat. If you make the effort to link several cages together and customize them inside, your pet will be able to roam, tunnel, climb, burrow, and stash to his heart's content. (See the section "Add-ons.")

When choosing a hamster habitat, here are a few points to keep in mind. First, make sure to match habitat to hamster. Don't buy a setup designed for a dwarf hamster if you plan to purchase a larger Syrian hamster. And don't buy a round module unless it's to be part of an extensive cage system—hamsters often become disorientated and stressed when they can't find corners to hide in, to store food in, or to use as a bathroom.

Plastic cage units need to be checked for adequate ventilation; they should have enough holes or slots for good air circulation. And, if you live in a hot climate and don't have air-conditioning, opt for wire or combination wire/plastic units instead of all-plastic ones. Your little Hammie will breathe easier. Whatever type of module you buy, be sure that the door opening is large enough for you to get your hand in to pick up your pet. Then test the door itself to see that it closes securely. It does? Now it's up to you to check that the door is properly latched each time you close it. Otherwise, it won't be long before you have a four-legged furball on the loose.

Some hamster enthusiasts find hamster habitats hard to clean—the more extensive the setup, the more time-consuming it is to take apart and wash. (Bottle brushes work wonders in the tubes.) The other BIG disadvantage is that some hamsters gnaw through and escape from these habitats. So, if you buy one, check it frequently for signs of tooth action and replace any damaged parts pronto. (Check the section "Plastic cage headaches . . . and solutions" in Chapter 5 for more information.)

Wire cages

Wire cages have many advantages. They provide great ventilation,

Combination wire/plastic cages are colorful and comfy.

they're easy to customize by attaching accessories to the cage wire, and they're readily available in pet shops. But are they all suitable for hamsters? In a word, no. To start with, many wire hamster cages are too small. At least they are if used on their own. However, by purchasing cage door adapters, you can link several cages together with tubes in much the same way as hamster habitats are joined together. Or, you can link a wire cage to a hamster habitat system. This multimodule route is a good way to go. Why? Because an extended layout gives Hammie plenty of roam room. When using a cage door adapter, make sure it fits the doorway snugly and doesn't leave room for your hamster to wiggle through. Check it frequently for gnaw damage, too, and replace if necessary.

There's no problem with air circulation in a wire cage. Notice the full floors on the upper levels of this model—they're a good safety feature.

Is your apartment too small for a multimodule setup? Then look for a multilevel wire cage instead. But buy one made for hamsters. Otherwise, the bars might be too far apart, and your pet could escape. Take your measuring tape to the store and measure the space between the bars. For dwarf hamsters, the spacing should be no more than 3/16 inch (0.5 cm). For Syrians, the spacing should be no more than 3/8 inch (1.0 cm). Next, take a look at the upper levels of the cage. Does the cage you like come equipped with narrow platforms or with full floors? Platforms are a bad idea. Hamsters have poor depth perception and can fall off them. Instead, choose a cage that has full floors on the upper levels . . . it will be safer for your pet.

Unfortunately, second-story floors are usually made of wire—not good for your pet's tootsies. A wire floor can be made easier on the feet by covering it completely with Magic Mat from Oasis (found in pet stores) or plastic needlepoint canvas (found in craft stores). These coverings can be cut to fit and attached to the floor or sides of the cage with twist ties. For added comfort, pile on soft nesting material.

It's not just the construction of the upper stories you have to worry about; you need to inspect the ground floor, too. Nowadays, the base or ground floor of the cage is

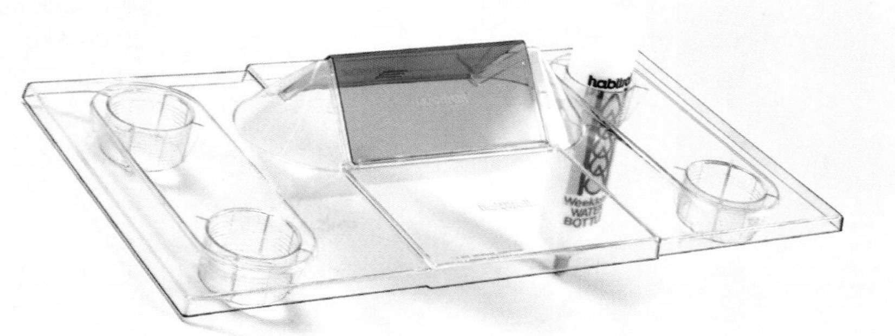

Use a special topper to connect a stand-alone aquarium to other modules.

usually plastic, but sometimes there's a wire insert covering the floor. Because walking on wire day after day can injure a hamster's delicate feet, you need to remove that wire insert.

Hamsters love to climb, and a wire cage with horizontal bars gives them ample opportunity to exercise their little legs. However, there are differing opinions as to whether or not scaling the cage wires is a safe activity. Although hopping up the bars is great exercise, accidents can happen and even a short fall can cause an injury. If you're worried about this, get a cage with vertical bars that can't be climbed, and provide ladders or tubes for climbing.

Aquariums

Aquariums are readily available and can often be picked up cheaply at a garage sale or a flea market. You might even have an old aquarium gathering dust in the basement after the goldfish died. Will it make a suitable hamster home?

On the plus side, your hamster can't gnaw through a glass aquarium like he can through a plastic cage, and he can't kick his bedding out onto the floor like he can in a wire cage. On the downside, aquariums are not well ventilated. In the summer or in a hot room, your hamster could roast in a hot aquarium or even suffer heatstroke. Poor ventilation can also lead to a buildup of ammonia fumes inside the aquarium. These fumes, which are caused by a chemical breakdown of urine, can cause respiratory problems for a hamster unless you're diligent about cleanup. Talking about cleanup, another drawback to aquariums is that they're heavy to handle and awkward to clean.

A 10-gallon (40-L) tank is the minimum size for a hamster home, and even this size by itself isn't adequate. Your pet will be much better off if you make that 10-gallon (40-L) aquarium part of a larger cage system. How do you do this? Buy a plastic ventilated tank topper specifically designed to integrate a plain 10-gallon (40-L) aquarium into a

Customized with add-ons, this Safari setup makes a stimulating hamster habitat.

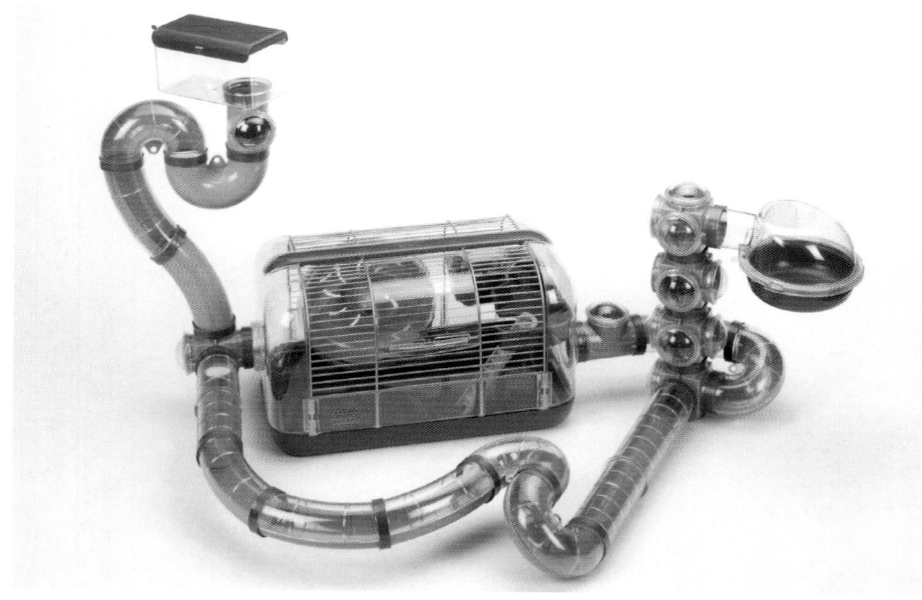

larger hamster habitat. Plastic habitat tubes are inserted through the round holes in the topper so that the aquarium can be linked up to modules, mazes, and more. Give your hamster an extended setup like this, and he'll be happy. Leave him confined to a glass box, and he'll very likely develop obsessive/compulsive behavior such as clawing at the glass, running back and forth endlessly, and eating the silicone sealant. Boredom for a hamster is a terrible thing.

Add-ons

Add-ons are those extras you purchase to make your hamster's living space more interesting for him. They can fit inside the cage, outside the cage, or link cages together. Add-ons and add-ins include tubes and tunnels, connectors, ladders, mazes, balconies, solariums, lookout towers, burrowing tanks, wheels, spinners, tree houses, and snack bars. The more add-ons you provide, the more stimulating an environment your hamster will have. But you don't need to blow your budget with one swipe of the debit card . . . save up a little each week and buy a new add-on when you can afford to.

When shopping for these accessories, make sure that what you buy fits what you already have—not all brands are interchangeable. Some items are made to clip onto cage wires; others come with suction cups that attach to plastic or glass walls.

Make sure that the add-ons that join module to module are connected properly. Leave no openings for a hamster escape artist! And, wherever a lid is part of the add-on (for example, on sky restaurants, towers, tree houses, or mazes), make sure that it's held on securely. Some lids snap/lock into place. Others will need to be taped down with packing tape to prevent your hamster from lifting the lid and going AWOL.

Don't think of add-ons and add-ins as optional extras. They're necessary for your hamster's physical and mental well-being. Scuttling through tunnels, digging in a burrowing tank, running on a wheel, stashing food in out-of-the-way corners . . . all of these activities keep your hamster fit, healthy, and interested in life.

Location

Where in your house are you going to put that hamster cage? This is a question that needs careful thought. During the day, when hamsters sleep, they need total peace and quiet. If their sleep is disturbed, they become stressed, and stress often leads to health problems. Although hamsters can clamp their ears shut when they sleep, they have a very acute sense of hearing, and noises that don't bother you will bother them. So pick a quiet spot for the cage. Don't stick it next to a stereo system, a subwoofer, or a TV that's on in the daytime. And don't vacuum around the cage when Hammie's asleep. Keep it away from noisy, vibrating appliances like dishwashers and washing machines. And keep it away from appliances that cycle on and off like refrigerators, furnaces, air conditioners, or freezers. The cage shouldn't be near drafts or a heat source, and it shouldn't be in bright light—this means no direct sunlight by day and no halogen lights at night.

These are the no-no's of cage location from the hamster's point of view; now for your point of view. Unless you're a *very* sound sleeper or you work the night shift, it's not a good idea to share your bedroom with a hamster. Hamsters are nocturnal. They're up and running during the night. You won't want to have your beauty sleep disturbed at 3:00 A.M. when Hammie's racking up the miles on his wheel.

So where is a good location for the hamster cage? No one spot is perfect for every household. Where you put the cage depends upon your unique home environment. The bottom line is find a good, quiet daytime location for your hamster's home and leave it there.

Bedding do's and don'ts

For a hamster, you'll need to get two different types of bedding. There's the bedding that covers the bottom of the cage and also the soft

Pick your pet's bedding with care . . . look for good absorbency and good odor control.

nesting material that goes into sleep areas.

For the cage bottom, you're looking for comfy bedding that will absorb the hamster's urine. Although hamsters don't piddle all over the cage, the corner or corners where they do urinate can get quite smelly. So, odor control and good absorbency should come first . . . softness is an added plus.

The most popular bedding choice is wood shavings. However, not all shavings are created equal. Stay away from pine and cedar shavings. These contain phenol, a chemical that can cause respiratory problems and possible liver damage in small animals. Hardwood, such as aspen, is the wood of choice for shavings. The problem with wood shavings is that they're not particularly absorbent. Your hamster's cage could get pretty wet and stinky unless you clean out the soiled corners daily or potty train your pet (see Chapter 6).

Other wood-based products make better bedding than shavings. For example, CareFRESH, which is made from wood pulp waste, looks like shredded egg cartons and is a real winner in the softness department. It's also nontoxic, biodegradable, and more absorbent than shavings. Pile it up 3 or 4 inches (7 to 10 cm) deep and watch Hammie have fun burrowing through it.

Then there are chipped wood products like Sani-chips. Made from aspen or hard maple, these chips are absorbent, fresh smelling, soft on the feet, and ideal for burrowing through. Their only drawback is that they scatter everywhere, though this is not a problem in an aquarium or plastic habitat.

For great absorbency, you can't beat wood pellets. In this category, pine is a possibility so long as it has been heat-treated to remove the phenols. Feline Pine and Pine Fresh are names to look for, with All Pet

Pine being similar but softer. Or check out the odor-eating aspen pellets like Barnaby Farms Pet Bedding and Gentle Touch Pet Bedding, which do a super job of soaking up urine and controlling odors.

Never use sawdust as bedding, even if you know it's come from hardwood. It's much too dusty and could be a problem for a hamster's respiratory system.

Pellets made from recycled newspaper such as Yesterday's News, Kitty Soft, and Sheppard & Greene are becoming popular. These paper pellets are nontoxic and biodegradable, and don't scatter easily. However, they tend to be somewhat dusty and don't do quite such a good job of odor control as the wood pellets. They are also a bit hard on hamster feet, so try to find the softer paper products like Cell-Sorb Plus or Yesterday's News soft-texture. Whatever you do, don't line the cage with your daily newspaper . . . it's nonabsorbent, it stays smelly, and the ink rubs off onto Hammie's fur.

What about beddings made from grains and grass? Corncob is the most readily available. You can find it everywhere. Stick to the unscented kind because strong odors like perfume and chlorophyll make many hamsters sick. Corncob bedding is inexpensive, soft on the feet, and great for burrowing. However, when used in aquariums, it can get moldy if not changed frequently. Other grass and grain beddings come in pelleted form. Look for Cat Works (grain) and Critter Country (grass). Both are biodegradable and nontoxic, and they get a high rating for odor control and absorbency.

So, out of all the choices, what bedding is best for Hammie? There is no clear-cut answer. The bedding you choose may be a matter of trial and error. For example, some hamsters are allergic to some bedding. If you find your pet lying on his back and panting when you know the cage is not too hot, maybe it's the bedding that's affecting his breathing. Change to a totally different type.

Is your hamster living in an extended cage setup? Then you might want to use two different types of bedding. Try heaping up a deep layer of CareFRESH or aspen shavings for burrowing fun in one section and use a thin layer of wood pellets everywhere else. Lucky Hammie!

Now on to nesting material. Think of this as your hamster's fluffy comforter. He needs it wherever he sleeps. Hamsters don't just curl up in a corner to sleep; they like a small,

A ceramic sleep house stands up to tooth attacks.

A coconut cabana, either store-bought or homemade, makes a great hamster hangout.

enclosed area in which to snooze. Always have a sleep house somewhere in the cage. Ceramic ones are best because they can't be chewed, but wood, plastic, or woven grass houses will do as long as you're prepared to replace them from time to time. Add-on accessories such as lookout towers, tree houses, or sky restaurants are often commandeered by hamsters as sleep houses, too.

Tissues or toilet paper make fine nesting material . . . let your pet shred his own.

A coconut cabana makes a unique, all-natural, and cozy sleep house. If you're into do-it-yourself projects, you can even make your own by drilling a 2-inch (5-cm) hole in a large coconut then scooping out the flesh. (See photo.) Or, for dwarf hamsters, here's another cheap and easy D-I-Y project for a comfy bunkhouse. Take a six-pack, cardboard egg carton, close the lid, and cut an entrance hole at one end. If you leave a pile of nesting material by the entry, your pint-sized pet can drag some in just in time for his next nap.

Sleeping quarters need to be stuffed with nesting material because a hamster likes to snuggle right in. Paper products are the safest choice. Try Eco-Bedding, Super Pet Carnival of Crinkles, plain shredded paper strips (no ink) from a paper shredder, pieces of paper towel, torn tissues, or strips of toilet paper. CareFRESH bedding also makes great nesting material, as does timothy hay.

Although the hamster fluff available at pet shops looks cozy, it's best to pass it up. The same goes for fabric, felt, cotton batting, polyester stuffing, and cotton balls. These materials can be swallowed and cause internal blockage, they can get stuck in hamster cheek pouches, and the long stringy bits can get wound around hamster feet and legs. Coconut fiber bedding is another no-no—the fibers are sharp and can cut footpads.

Nutrition

Nutrition for your pet is easy. For the main menu, it's hamster seed mixes, small animal lab blocks, or a combination of both. Seed mixes really appeal to a hamster's palette—he can pick and choose what he wants. And, unfortunately, that's exactly what he'll do, pigging out on the fatty sunflower seeds and turning up his nose at the rest. With blocks, on the other hand, he gets a well-rounded diet with each mouthful. To provide both good nutrition and good taste, perhaps the best plan is to dish up blocks on a daily basis and supplement them with a tastier seed mix a couple of times a week.

Always buy small packages and check the *Best Before* dates. Hamsters aren't big eaters, and the food will last for a long time. When a bag's been opened, transfer the food to an airtight container and store it in a cool, dry place.

How often do you feed your hamster? Hamsters eat free choice, so fill his dish and leave him to it. He'll eat when he's hungry. He'll also pack his pouches and stash food in different corners of the cage modules, in his sleep house, in the burrowing tank, or anywhere else that strikes his fancy.

Round out Hammie's diet with fruits and vegetables. Serve these up in small portions because large helpings will give him diarrhea. He'll enjoy tiny pieces of celery, carrots, broccoli, peas, cabbage, apples, plums, figs, pears, cut grapes, strawberries, and melon. But no citrus fruit, please—Hammie can't handle the citric acid. And no dried fruits—they can get stuck in his cheek pouches. Greens and grasses can also add variety to your pet's diet. Dandelions, sorrel, clover, timothy hay, Herbal Hay, and alfalfa are all good choices. You can even grow your own hamster grass; kits are available at pet stores. Any fresh produce given to your pet must be well washed and free of chemicals. And fresh food that's stashed in corners should be cleaned out before it spoils.

A hamster stuffs his cheek pouches with food . . .

. . . look how big they can get.

Hamster grass! Yum, yum . . . gimme some.

Hamsters need a diet high in carbohydrates, so dish up cooked pasta or rice, sugar-free cereal, and whole-wheat bread. Again, small amounts only, please. Extra protein can come from tiny tastes of cottage cheese or yogurt, or from tidbits of cooked chicken, fish, or beef. For a special gourmet delight, bring out a mealworm or two once a day. Yep, hamsters love 'em. Serve them up with tweezers if you're too squeamish to pick them up with your fingers. Where do you find this culinary delight? Most pet shops stock them.

Crunch, crunch . . . a tasty wafer cake is nutritious, too.

For treats, tickle Hammie's taste buds with yogurt drops, yogurt dips or chips, seed sticks, hamster Party Cakes, or one of the dozens of hamster treats on the pet shop shelves. There are Krunch A Rounds, Nutrapuffs, Chew Biscuits, Nibblers, Healthy Bits, Healthy Hearts and Veggie Burgers, Fruity Clouds, Little Kisses, Carrot or Corn Slims, Small Animal Waffles and Cakes, Lofty's, or Rondis . . . and many more besides. Skip sugary people sweets—no cakes, cookies, or chocolate. And keep in mind that treats are just that, treats. Give them sparingly.

Because hamsters need more salt than is found in their food, you need to provide a salt lick or a mineral/salt block somewhere in the cage. You'll find different kinds available, along with different kinds of hangers. (See photo.)

One last word on nutrition. To wash down all this good food, water is a must. Have fresh water available 24 hours a day. Are you concerned about the quality of your tap water or well water? Is it high in chlorine, iron, or sulfur? You might want to provide filtered or bottled water instead.

Put a salt lick in your pet's cage so that he gets the sodium he needs.

Bottles and bowls

Your hamster needs fresh water, but how fresh will it stay if you serve it in a bowl? Think what else might make its way into the bowl . . . food, droppings, bedding. In fact, in hamster cages at pet shops, it's not uncommon to see water bowls so full of soggy bedding that there's no water left. Don't let this happen in your pet's cage—buy a water bottle instead of a bowl.

Choose the water bottle with care. It needs to be leak proof and as gnaw proof as possible. To avoid leaks, look for a sipper bottle with double ball bearings. Can't find one? Then, take your pick of what's available and ask to try before you buy. Fill the bottle right up to the top with water to create a vacuum, turn it upside down, and inspect the sipper tube. If it drips, forget it; if it doesn't drip, buy it.

Gnawing is another matter. Hamsters can chew through plastic in no time, and a water bottle is a prime target for a bored hamster. Look for bottles with rounded edges—a hamster's sharp little chompers can't get a good grip on them. Or, invest in a metal protector that shields the plastic bottle from tooth attacks. Pay particular attention to the sipper tube; it must be made of metal. Glass can be broken and plastic can be nibbled—neither is safe.

There are sipper bottles available for wire cages (attach with a wire hanger or a bracket), for aquariums (attach with suction cups), and for plastic hamster habitats (attach with suction cups or an adhesive-backed bracket). In some habitats, the bottle fits right through a hole in the cage top. This is a convenient setup for most hamsters, but the sipper tube might not hang down low enough for a baby or dwarf hamster. Always make sure your pet can reach the bottle and is actually drinking from it.

A ceramic food dish is tip proof and gnaw proof.

When you get the height right, don't just hang the bottle up and leave it. Even though your hamster doesn't drink much, it's important to change his water daily and to wash the bottle well while you're at it.

There's even more choice when it comes to food bowls. Small, heavy ceramic dishes are probably the most popular pick. Hammie can't tip one of these over. Nor can he tip over the bowls that lock onto wire cages or the ones that stick on to plastic habitats. But don't attach those bowls too high on the side of a cage—Hammie has short legs. As with water bottles, clean food bowls daily.

Hamsters are very meticulous housekeepers . . . they like a place for everything and everything in its place. So keep the food bowl and sipper bottle together in the dining area, well away from the sleep area and toilet facilities. And in an expansive cage system, don't make your hamster run far for a drink. Why not hang up one water bottle in his main villa and another in his garden gazebo?

Picking a potty

Did you know that your hamster can be litter trained? It's a great idea because it makes life in the cleanup lane much easier for you. You'll give it a try? Then right from the word "go," you'll need to place a potty in a corner of the cage. See Chapter 6 for the scoop on both store-bought and homemade potties.

Veterinarian visits

When you make a hamster part of the family, it's unlikely that you'll have to dig too deeply into your pocket to pay veterinary bills. Hamsters don't need yearly vaccinations, they don't need neutering or spaying, and many medical procedures that are routinely performed on larger animals are not practical for minimammals. However, like any other pet, your hamster can get sick. Keep a hamster care book on hand so you'll know what symptoms to watch for. With such a small pet, it's important to call a veterinarian the moment you notice that your pet's out of sorts. Don't take a wait-and-see attitude . . . this could be fatal. And don't wait until your hamster's ill before trying to find a vet. Not all veterinarians know all there is to know about hamsters. Call around and find one who is hamster savvy *before* the need arises.

Chapter Two

Hamster-Hunting Homework

Choosing a trainee

Now that everything's ready at home, the big moment has arrived. It's hamster-shopping time. But where are you going to do your shopping? For convenience, most people go the pet store route. In fact, it's a good idea to visit several shops. This way, you'll have a wider variety of hamsters to pick and choose from, and you can compare the hamsters' living quarters as well. The cages should be clean, sizable, and uncrowded. They should contain suitable bedding as well as fresh food and water. Is there a sleep house in the cage? That's a bonus for daytime snoozing. Is the cage lighting suitably subdued? Hamsters can get stressed-out and sick if kept under hot, bright lights.

In a good pet shop, knowledgeable staff will take time to give you advice and answer your questions. However, some hamster hunters prefer dealing directly with breeders. Why? Breeders usually specialize in colors and fur types you won't find at the pet store. And, breeders often hand tame the babies. This is a big plus because the earlier a hamster is handled, the better pet it becomes.

Evening is the best time to pick your pupil(s)

In their natural habitat, hamsters sleep in underground tunnels during the day. What better way to avoid predators? At night, they roam arid countryside foraging for food. Pet hamsters keep the same hours . . . they sleep during the day and explore at night. So think about it. Does it make sense to choose your hamster during the day? Of course not! At best, she'll be half-awake; at worst, she'll bite you for disturbing her sleep. Always wait until late afternoon or evening to pick your pupil. At this time of day, the group will be up and about, lively and energetic; their true personalities will come shining through.

Pick your pet in the evening when she's wide-awake.

Does the species make a difference?

There are basically two types of hamsters sold as pets—the larger Syrian hamsters and the smaller dwarf hamsters. Syrian hamsters (a.k.a. Golden, Fancy, Standard, or Teddy Bear) are widely available. Walk into any pet shop and you should find a great selection. Syrians come in solid colors like gold, cream, black, gray, cinnamon, sable, and white. They also come in variegated colors like tortoiseshell (black and golden brown) and calico (black/golden brown/white). Patterns add another twist . . . look for banded (white band around the middle), dominant spot (spotted), and roan (looks white but is ticked with darker hairs). Then there are coat types to consider . . . shorthaired, longhaired (sometimes called Teddy Bear or Angora), satin (plush like velvet), and rex (wavy and velvety).

The most popular dwarf hamster—the Dwarf Russian—comes in two different species, the Campbell's Russian and the Winter White Russian. So far, so good. Where it gets confusing is that they're both sometimes called Siberian or Djungarian hamsters, and you might not be able to find out which species you're actually buying. However, whatever they're called, both species are good-natured and easier to handle than other dwarf hamsters.

More difficult to find, and more difficult to train, are the Chinese Dwarf and the Roborovski Dwarf hamsters. The Chinese Dwarfs tend to be aggressive, the Roborovskis are tiny and timid; they're both fast, jumpy, hard to handle, and hard to catch. Although they are endlessly fascinating to watch, they're not easy to tame.

A Golden Syrian is a popular pick.

So for training purposes, which hamster is the best bet? If there are children in the family, go for a Syrian hamster. They're larger, not so fast, and easier to get (and keep) hold of. Being loners, they don't bond with other hamsters, so they'll be more likely to bond with you, especially if you work at it. Do you have your heart set on dwarf hamsters? Then stick to Dwarf Russians . . . they make better people pets.

Fuzzy Figment is a Teddy Bear Syrian.

Male or female?

Do you want a male or a female for a pet? Does it matter? Not really. Males have a stronger body odor and tend to become obese with old age . . . gotta watch that diet. However, for pet purposes and for training purposes, there's not much difference between the sexes . . . it's the personality of the individual hamster that counts.

Young or old?

Most pet shops have cages full of hamsters at different ages and stages. Should you lean toward an older one or a younger one when picking your pet? If possible, choose one that's three to four weeks old, just weaned, and ready to face life on its own. When hamster/human bonding begins at this impressionable age, it's usually very successful. A young hamster that's handled frequently learns that people are part of her life. An older hamster that hasn't had this interaction usually doesn't become as tame and people tolerant.

Trainability isn't the only reason for buying a young hamster. Hamsters don't live long. If you buy an older one, your time together will be short. If you buy a baby, you'll make the most of your hamster's two- to three-year life span.

Dwarf hamsters need dwarf-sized equipment.

These young Syrian hamsters will soon need to be housed separately.

Another advantage to buying a three- to four-week-old hamster is that it's unlikely to be pregnant; female hamsters can start breeding when they're just 35 days old. So buy from a place where the staff know how to sex hamsters and where the sexes are kept in separate cages. Otherwise, you might end up with more hamsters than you paid for! In fact, before you buy *any* hamster, it's a good idea to ask about the store's return policy . . . can you bring back any babies you hadn't bargained on? Remember, if you can't return them and you can't palm them off on your friends, you'll have to house each and every one in a separate cage when they're a few weeks old.

One or more?

When you see hamsters at the pet shop, you'll probably see lots of them hanging out in the same cage. Does this mean that group living is the way to go? Can you keep three or four hamsters in the same habitat at home? If they are Syrians, the answer is a definite "no." Syrians are loners, they're very territorial, and they *must* be housed separately. The only reason they're caged together at the pet shop is that they're young. For the first five or six weeks of life, Syrians can live in harmony. After that, it's every hamster for itself. Left together, they'll fight . . . possibly to the death. Are you still determined to have more than one Syrian? Then it's separate cages, separate playtime, separate everything.

The story *can* be different for dwarf hamsters. Sometimes they are kept together in pairs or groups (same sex, please, or you'll have a hamster population explosion). Those housed together don't have to come from the same litter, but they should be roughly the same age and size, and they should be introduced to one another early in life. Also, the cage needs to be big enough so that the individual hamsters can go off on their own when they need to be alone.

However, shared accommodations don't always work out. As they get older, some dwarf hamsters become less sociable and declare war on their former buddies. After eight or nine months, they might have to be put into separate cages. If you buy more than one dwarf, be prepared for this possibility.

Pick a happy, healthy hamster

When buying a hamster, look for one that's healthy. How can you tell? Your choice should have clear, bright eyes and a shiny coat with no bald spots. Avoid any hamsters that are sneezing or sniffling. Check that there are no discharges from the eyes, ears, nose, or anus. In fact, any wetness and matted fur around the tail area could be a sign of wet tail, a serious illness that hamsters develop when stressed. Next, look at the hamster's teeth when it yawns. Make sure those teeth are not broken or crooked. Crooked teeth can cause problems down the road.

Pick a pet that's lively and energetic rather than one that's cowering in a corner. Be aware of body language—a hamster that's jumping around, stretching and yawning, sniffing and looking curious is a good bet. A hamster that's growling, gnashing her teeth, or lying on her back, teeth bared, is best left for someone else. What *you* want is a pet with an A+ personality.

Bright-eyed and alert, Fudge is a picture of health.

Chapter Three

Teach Your Hamster to Welcome Your Touch

Hamsters can be afraid of people

As pets go, hamsters haven't been part of human families for very long because they weren't brought out of the wild and into cages until the 1930s. For this reason, hamsters aren't as comfortable around humans as other animals are. Then, there's the fact that, in the wild, hamsters are loners—it's not part of their nature to form bonds.

What does this mean for you as an owner? It means that you and your hamster probably won't become best buddies over night. You'll have to work at getting your hamster to like you.

Early education is best

"The earlier, the better" should be your motto when it comes to training your pet hamster. As you learned in the last chapter, a young hamster, three to four weeks old, is at an impressionable age and ready to learn. Seize the moment! Start handling that youngster every day—several times a day—and he'll soon accept you as part of his life.

Hamsters that aren't handled frequently from a young age develop solitary habits. They don't become hooked on humans and often don't welcome the human touch. Most biters fall into this category. Some older hamsters *can* be taught to like people, but you'll have to be persistent and consistent, and it takes time. If you're a first-time hamster owner, or if the hamster is to be a child's pet, make things easy for everybody . . . buy a young one.

Homecoming hints

The great day has arrived! It's homecoming time for Horatio. However, what's an exciting time for you can be a stressful time for your new pet. Think about the move from his point of view. He's leaving familiar faces and places to go live with strangers in a new environment. This is enough to have a hamster knocking at the knees, and a stressed hamster can soon become a sick hamster. Many hamsters develop a potentially fatal illness called wet tail as a result of change or disruption in their lives. How? First, change causes stress, then stress upsets the delicate balance of bacteria in the intestinal tract. This, in turn, causes diarrhea and then dehydration. If you see any sign of wetness around your pet's rump area, take him to the vet *immediately*. But prevention is better than cure . . . to keep your pet out of the hamster hospital, make his change of address as hassle-free as possible.

First give careful thought to the trip home. No handheld Horatios, please! A small pet carrier is a must. The pet store will probably provide you with a cardboard transport box, but such a flimsy container might not stand up to the gnawing of hamster teeth. You're better off taking along your own small, sturdy cardboard box or shoe box with some air holes poked in the top. Also bring along some masking tape or rubber bands to secure the lid to the box so that your new pet can't nudge the lid up with his nose and escape. Better yet, in case the hamster starts nibbling through the cardboard at the air holes, stick the small cardboard box into a deep plastic storage box. Then, if your new pet manages to gnaw through the small box, he won't be able to make a quick getaway into the car upholstery. At the store, ask for some of the used bedding from the cage that your hamster was housed in, and toss it into the cardboard box. Hamsters have an acute sense of smell, and if your pet is surrounded with familiar scents on the way home, he'll be much more at ease.

This young hamster is looking to you for training!

Is your trip home a long one? Then forget the cardboard boxes; you take a risk of Horatio gnawing his way through before you're halfway home. Instead, invest in a small wire or plastic travel cage, and put in lots of nesting material so the little guy can hide.

When Horatio's ready for the road, go straight home—don't cruise the aisles at the pet store, don't stop off for a quick grocery run on the way home, don't drop in at grandma's so she can "ooh" and "ahh." Your new pet won't appreciate the noise and commotion . . . he'll be frightened and overwhelmed. A quiet, peaceful car ride is what he needs. So no loud music, no poking fingers, and NO getting Horatio out of the box. What you *can* do is speak softly to him so that bonding begins.

A small pet carrier makes the ride home safe and comfortable.

When you get to your house, take Horatio straight to his new house. Of course, getting him out of that travel box and into the cage could be tricky. He might be a tad upset, he might be fearful, he might be defensive . . . in other words, anything but cooperative. So play it safe. To avoid a possible bite, put on a pair of gardening gloves before transferring Horatio from box to cage. Cup both hands around his stocky body, and *gently* place him into his new home. Toss in some of that used-at-the-pet-shop bedding to give his new quarters a familiar smell. Then leave him undisturbed. Go about your own business while he goes about the business of exploring his new residence. He'll want to find his food and water, investigate his sleep house, mark his toilet area, and perhaps even take a whirl on his wheel.

For the next two days, have patience. Leave Horatio alone so that he can get over the stress of the move. You can watch him, but don't touch him just yet. Don't reach into the habitat except to change food and water and to scoop out soiled bedding. Don't jostle the cage, don't make noise around the cage, and don't invite the neighbor kids over to gawk. Do, however, stand close to the cage and talk reassuringly to your new pet (a.k.a. the newbie) at frequent intervals. It's by your smell and the sound of your voice that he gets to know you.

Besides leaving Horatio alone for a day or two, there are a couple of other things that you can do to help him cope with moving stress. First, to maintain the body's correct chemical balance, try to get some electrolytes into him by offering Gatorade, Pedialyte, or Powerade. Second, to help restore the balance of the natural bacteria in his intestinal tract, put 1 teaspoon (5 mL) of yogurt into a feeding dish and place it beside his food. Do this in the evening when he's active and hungry.

After Horatio has been left to himself for a couple of days, and after he's had a nutritional power boost, he should have settled in. How will you know if he has? When he yawns, stretches, and starts grooming in a relaxed manner, you'll know he's feeling at home.

DO NOT DISTURB

From the get-go, it's important to understand your pet's need for daytime peace and quiet. In the wild, hamsters roam the countryside at night then replenish their energy by sleeping deeply during the day. For

Horatio to stay healthy, his cage life needs to mimic the life of his forefathers—he can't be reprogrammed to fit your family's schedule.

So your motto needs to be "Let sleeping hamsters lie." *Never*, *never*, *never* disturb your furball when he's snoozing. If your pet's sleep is frequently disturbed, he'll become stressed, and stress leads to health problems. In fact, the stress caused by waking a hamster from a sound sleep can significantly shorten his life span. What's more, a rudely awoken hamster can be a grouchy hamster, and a grouchy hamster often bites. Don't blame your hamster; it's just his natural response to a rude awakening. After all, would you be bright eyed and bushy tailed if you were hauled out of a deep sleep every night? Well, for a hamster that keeps night-shift hours, it's daytime disturbance that's the no-no. So don't keep yanking Horatio out of his cage during the day, and make sure the kids understand and follow this rule.

Remember too, it's not just people that can disturb Horatio's beauty sleep—household noises can also jolt him awake. Go back to the "Location" section in Chapter 1 to refresh your memory about noises to be avoided. And to help your pet get a good day's sleep, why not cover his cage with a blanket or towel?

Handling how-to

Just like you, your hamster won't always sleep eight hours straight . . . sometimes you might see Horatio toddling around for short periods of time during the day. This, however, is not the time to start handling sessions. Wait until evening for the best chance of success; wait until Horatio is wide-awake and ready for action. Be aware, too, that a hamster's body language can tell you whether or not he's in the mood for being handled. If he's lying back baring his incisors, if he's growling, squeaking, or grinding his teeth . . . forget it. If he's loafing around, eating, stretching, and grooming . . . go to it.

Then the training strategy is to take things in easy stages. You can't rush a hamster into liking you. You have to build his trust and confidence in you, one step at a time. You also have to realize that hamsters don't have the best eyesight in the world. It's not your good looks that Horatio's going to recognize; it's your smell and the sound of your voice that he'll commit to memory. For this reason, you focus on those two senses in your handling sessions.

The first step in handling is to introduce the newbie to your hand . . . but not a hand that's just been shoveling in supper. Fingers that smell of food could invite an unwelcome nip. So, wash your hands with unscented soap, and rinse them well to get rid of any food smells. Next, try a little trick that seasoned hamster handlers use. Rub your hands with some of Horatio's used nesting material or bedding so that he recognizes that familiar Eau de Hamster. Then slowly slide your hand into the cage, taking care not to startle the resident. Don't chase after him with your hand, and don't wiggle your fingers . . . let him make the first move. Hamsters are curious critters, and yours is unlikely to be an exception. Watch him sniff your fingers—what he's doing is filing your smell away into his scent memory for future reference. And if all the while you talk to him in a pleasant tone, he'll file away the sound of your voice as well.

Is your hamster a bit defensive when you intrude into his space? Are you afraid that your hand will be bitten rather than sniffed? It's OK to wear garden gloves rubbed in used bedding until you and your pet have learned to trust one another.

Keep the initial encounter short, but repeat it several times an evening for a few days or until your pet's treating your hand as part of the cage furniture. Now it's on to handling step number two. Get out the treats! Then when it's time to put your hand into the cage again, don't go in empty-handed. Pick up a sunflower seed or a yogurt drop between forefinger and thumb, and offer the treat to your furball. The idea here is to get Horatio to associate your hand and your scent with good things. When he's comfortable taking food from your fingers, place the treat onto your flat palm instead. Why? Horatio will have to climb aboard your hand to get his reward, and this gets him used to being handheld. It lets him know that your hand is nothing to be afraid of.

Cupped in your hands, your pet will feel secure.

As soon as he willingly walks onto your palm, it's time for step number three. While he's helping himself to his treat or sitting on your hand nibbling the goody, stroke your hamster gently a few times with the fingers of your other hand. Chances are, he'll be so busy with his treat that he'll hardly notice. When you get to the point that stroking Horatio's fur won't ruffle his feathers, it's on to step four . . . practicing the cup hold.

Get your hamster to climb onto the palm of your hand as before, but this time, cup your other hand loosely over the top of him. Let him see that hand coming . . . don't swoop it down from above or sneak it in from behind. If you do, he might think you're a predator and go into defensive mode (i.e., biting). What's the idea behind cocooning your hamster like this in your hands? Cupping him with both hands is how you get him out of the cage and how you hold him safely. But you have to practice the cup hold in the cage so Horatio won't be frightened of it.

Wait a minute, though. What do you do if the cage opening is too

Get your hamster used to the smell of your hand when it's young. (These youngsters will soon need to be housed in separate cages.)

small for you to get both hands in? Is it OK to take hold of Horatio by the scruff of his neck? The answer is "no." Even though scruffing can be done with one hand, it's not a good idea. Hamsters have lots of loose neck skin and can easily twist around and bite the hand that holds them. So scrub the scruff hold. Instead, concentrate on cupping your pet with one hand the best way you can.

The last step (whew . . . about time!) is to lift the cupped Horatio out of his cage and cradle him against your body. When held this way, he'll feel secure, and he won't be able to jump from your hands and possibly injure himself. He might, however, urinate on your hands the first few times he's held. Don't be alarmed. It's quite common for hamsters to piddle when they're frightened. If your pet seems afraid, nestle him close to your heart so he hears your heartbeat—this works wonders to calm a nervous or skittish pet.

Does this handling how-to sound like a lot of work? Well, it can be. Although some hamsters take to humans fairly quickly, others need weeks to warm to their owners. But however long it takes, it's time well spent because the more time you spend working with your hamster at an early age, the better, more people friendly pet he'll be. Teaching your hamster to trust you and like you is the most important training task you'll do. So be patient and be consistent. Before you know it, you and your buddy will have forged a rewarding relationship.

Beware of heights

Hamsters and heights don't mix. Don't be fooled by the furriness and stockiness of your hamster's body—it's more fracture prone than it looks. Even a short fall can cause serious injury or death. So, one basic rule of hamster handling has to be *keep your hamster away from heights.* This means that when you're holding Horatio, you need to sit rather than stand, and the lower to the ground the better. Sitting right on the floor is the best plan. But if the old bones aren't willing or able, try perching on a footstool or on several cushions. Sitting well back on a sofa is another option. Then, if Horatio shoots out of your grasp, he's likely to land on the sofa rather than crashing to the floor.

Here's another good idea, especially for the first few handling sessions. Why don't you and Horatio retire to the bathtub? Put in the plug, spread out a thick towel, climb in, and sit down—you've just found the perfect practice place. There are several advantages to this setup. One, your hamster can't fall because you're sitting down. Two, he can't make a quick getaway because he can't jump over the sides of the tub. Three, you can alternate handling time with free-roam time. And four, he's right at hand when you want to put him back into his cage. Tub sessions like this are a great way to introduce children to their new pet, especially a pet that can move like greased lightning and jump unexpectedly.

If, heaven forbid, your hamster is ever dropped, keep an eye on him for signs of discomfort. Any limping, dragging, difficulty in walking, or change in activity level, and he needs to go to the veterinarian right away.

Family focus

A hamster that's going to be a family pet needs to be introduced to everyone in the family at an early age. If you don't take the time to do this, chances are that Horatio will bond with some members of the family but not with others. He might not tolerate being touched by anyone whose scent and sound he hasn't memorized. In fact, even if Horatio has committed Dad's voice and smell to memory, he might not take to Dad. Not all hamsters like all people equally; some have definite people preferences.

If your family is like most families, everyone will be anxious to handle the newbie right away and all at once. This could be a recipe for disaster. An overwhelmed Horatio could start biting out of fear. So it's up to you as a responsible pet owner to exercise crowd control. You need to make sure there's no fighting over Horatio, no grabbing for him, no passing him back and forth . . . one handler at a time should be the golden rule.

Of course, when a young child is handling the family pet, another golden rule should be—supervise,

supervise, supervise! Hamsters are not lap dogs; they don't always cotton to cuddling. And children are champion cuddlers. They tend to treat their pets like stuffed animals, squeezing them much too enthusiastically. This could be a problem in more ways than one. First, the hamster could be hurt. It doesn't take much of a squeeze to harm a hamster. Second, no self-respecting hamster is going to put up with the squeeze treatment. The hamster squeezee will likely bite the child squeezer. Or, if he doesn't, it's a safe bet that he'll immediately try to escape the child's clutches, possibly being injured as he leaps to freedom. Third, an escaped hamster is hard for a child to catch. Fourth, Horatio has a memory like an elephant's. He won't forget who handled him roughly, and it's unlikely he'll bond with that child in the future.

Older children, as long as they're reliable, can be taught the hows, whats, whys, and wherefores of hamster care. Is Horatio going to be Paige and Taylor's pet? Then you'll have to give them a course in hamster basics. But even then, can you be sure that Paige will remember to clean the cage every Saturday or that Taylor will take time every day to handle Horatio? Will they still be sticking to their daily hamster chores after the novelty of the new pet has worn off? No matter what promises they make, most kids have a hard time following through with routine pet care, day after day after day. So, if your child has a hamster, you'll have to be the Pet Care Supervisor. You'll need to be the one in charge, making sure that the animal gets the care it needs and deserves.

Ten-year-old Kayla has learned the ins and outs of hamster care.

One of the joys of hamster ownership is showing off your furball to friends. Children especially get a kick out of this. But the question is, is it a good idea to let nonfamily members handle the hamster? Well, certainly not for the first few weeks. During this time, the focus should be strictly on the family. Later, when you know your hamster's nature, you'll have to decide whether or not his social skills are up to snuff. If your pet is well behaved, laid-back, and outgoing, then you can try introducing him to friends and neighbors. On the other hand, if he's a bit shy, nervous, or prone to nipping, then perhaps the best rule of thumb for nonfamily members should be look but don't touch.

Chapter Four
Knock, Knock, Who's There?

You called?

In the last chapter, you and your hamster were getting acquainted. You handled her on a daily basis and your patience has paid off—Frisbee trusts you and feels at ease with you. Now it's time for the next step in training . . . and that is to teach your pet to come when you want her. You need to be able to attract her attention without frightening her. If you just reach into the cage and grab your hamster without warning, she might be the one grabbing or nabbing you. Why? She'll think your big hand swooping down unexpectedly is a predator, and she's likely to bite you in self-defense. However, if you teach her to come to you rather than invading her space and scooping her up, she won't be frightened out of her wits.

Now the question is, how are you going to attract her attention? Just hovering around the cage and waving to her won't work . . . hamsters have poor eyesight. There's nothing wrong, however, with their hearing. So, when you want your pet to come running, why not try calling her by name?

Decide on the form of words that's going to be your calling card—for example, "Here Frisbee, Frisbee, Frisbee!"—and use the same words whenever you want your pet to sit up and take notice. Many hamsters are quick on the uptake . . . they learn to come right up to the cage doors when their owners call out a specific greeting. But what if your hamster turns a deaf ear when you say hello? Or, what if she responds when it suits her and ignores you when it doesn't? Then you need to train Frisbee to come to you using the old conditioned-response technique.

Conditioned response

Conditioned response? What's that? It's a training technique used by animal trainers to teach animals specific behaviors. For example, a rat can be taught to run a maze, a dog can learn to sit up and beg, or a ferret can be convinced to come to a squeaky toy. How does the technique work? It's really quite straightforward. You give a signal (the stimulus), your pet performs an action (the response), and then you give your pet a food reward (the reinforcement). In the following sections, you'll learn how to train your hamster to come to you whenever she hears a specific sound. But before you get started, you'll need to find a treat with guaranteed Frisbee appeal.

Your hamster will love her treats, but she shouldn't have too many.

The trick is in the treat

Food rewards (or treats) work wonders when training animals. So what scrumptious goodie will have your hamster drooling? Will it be a piece of raisin, part of a sunflower seed, or a bit of yogurt drop? How about a tiny tidbit of cheese, apple, cucumber, or strawberry? Check back to the "Nutrition" section in Chapter 1 for a listing of fruits, vegetables, and treats that appeal to the hamster palate. Then it's a matter of trial and error to find out just what tasty morsel tickles your hamster's fancy.

Does your pet act ho-hum about the rewards you're offering? Then here are two treat suggestions that smell enticing, taste delicious, and are irresistible to most hamsters. The first is Toob Snax for hamsters and gerbils, a cheese-flavored, squeezable snack in a tube. Fortified with vitamins and minerals, Toob Snax is a healthy treat for your pet. It squeezes out like toothpaste, and most hamsters will readily wolf down a 2- to 3-inch (5- to 7.5-cm) ribbon twice a day.

The second treat is Nutri-Cal, a vitamin supplement that comes in a tube. This product is more concentrated, so you can't offer much per day. The daily allowance of Nutri-Cal works out to 1/16 teaspoon (0.3 mL) per 6-ounce (170-g) Syrian hamster. However, if you have a 2-ounce (57-g) dwarf hamster, a dab or two a day is the max. Neither amount might sound like much, but you can dilute the Nutri-Cal with a little water to make it stretch. And remember, don't overdo any treat . . . your furball shouldn't be filling up on snacks and forgetting basic nutrition.

P.S. . . . Nutri-Cal is not only good as a treat, it's good to keep handy for hamster medical emergencies. If your pet gets sick and goes off her food, she'll often lap up the nutritious Nutri-Cal when she won't eat anything else. In fact, you can even mix medicine into it—the tasty flavor of the Nutri-Cal disguises the nasty flavor of the medicine. Check with your veterinarian about the proper use of vitamin supplements with a sick pet.

Call, knock, or whistle?

OK. You've figured out your hamster's favorite treat; now you have to figure out what sound will attract her attention. For many owners, a knocking sound does the trick. Knock gently on a surface next to the cage—the floor, the table, the bookshelf, the wall—or tap *lightly* on the cage itself. No hard knocks, please. Banging and thumping will frighten Frisbee and send her running to hide, just the opposite of what you're trying to achieve.

Another good sound would be a whistle, as long as it's person produced and not purchased. Your own low-toned whistle is fine. But store-bought ones are usually loud and shrill, and they are scary to sensitive hamster ears.

You can knock or whistle for free. But if you want to get high-tech, why not visit your local pet store and invest in one of the new clicker devices? Clicker training, or CT, is the latest rage in animal training. It's a new name for the old game of conditioned response, but with CT, you always use a clicker as the sound stimulus. For some hamsters, the click sound might be too loud. In that case, muffle the sound by putting the clicker into your pocket or into a thick sock.

Remember, *any* sound that's too loud or high-pitched can be frightening to a hamster. So don't use a clanging bell, an ear-splitting squeaky toy, or anything else that would have Frisbee covering her ears.

A little Nutri-Cal on a spoon will bring your pet running.

The plan of action

Don't start on your plan of action until your hamster trusts you completely and will eat from your hand. And don't ever wake her up for a training session. Wait until she's awake, alert, and playing around or grooming herself . . . in other words, sending out signals that she's happy and content. While you're waiting, divide up the treats into small bits so you don't fill her up with one treat. Then watch until she strays close to the cage wires or the cage door so that you can tempt her with a treat.

Now the timing is important. You want to knock, click, or whistle right at the moment she takes the treat so that she associates the sound with the food reward. At first, she'll come to you because she smells the treat. But with repeated practice, the sound itself (the knock) will be the stimulus that persuades her to perform the action (coming to you), which gets her the reward (the treat). Eventually, Frisbee will come running as soon as she hears the knock so that she can get the treat.

Repeat, repeat, repeat

Click-treat, click-treat, click-treat—every time you click or knock, make sure to give your pet a treat.

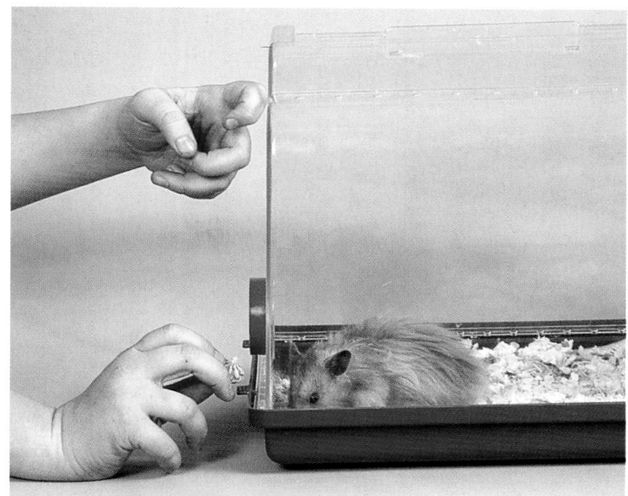

Knock, knock! Teach your hamster to answer your knock by offering her a treat.

And, repeat, repeat, repeat. It's repetition that ingrains the behavior, and practice makes perfect. But make the training sessions short and sweet. It's better to have several short sessions in an evening rather than one extended session because Frisbee's attention span isn't that long, and anyway, she shouldn't be overdosed on treats.

When your furball has mastered this behavior in the cage setting, work on getting her to come to you in the exercise area, too (see Chapters 8 and 9). After all, it's a lot easier to knock for your hamster when you want to get her than it is to go chasing after her. And, if Frisbee ever escapes from her cage, you increase the odds of finding her if she's been trained to come to a specific sound.

Chapter Five
Can Hamsters Be Trained Not to Gnaw?

Hamsters need to gnaw

Chomp, chomp, chew, chew—is your minimammal munching and crunching his way through life? Or, at least through his tube tunnels, his exercise wheel, his sky restaurant, and his sleep house? Don't get upset with Barney, he's not trying to get your goat. Gnawing is just part of his nature.

Hamsters need to gnaw. Have you ever taken a look at Barney's front teeth? They're whoppers. But that's nothing compared with the size they would be if he didn't keep gnawing. Hamsters have four front incisors, two on the top and two on the bottom, that keep growing throughout their lives. Gnawing is necessary to keep those teeth sharp and at the proper length. You can't train a hamster not to chew things, but here are a few strategies to limit the damage.

Chew sticks are made for gnawing.

Favorite targets

What's a hamster's favorite target when it comes to chewing? Almost anything in sight! Barney doesn't care what he wrecks as he goes about the business of keeping his teeth trimmed. With this in mind, you'll have to think carefully about the items you put into his cage. Use ceramic food dishes rather than plastic ones. Put the plastic water bottle into a metal protector. Or, buy a flat-back style that doesn't have any obvious edges for teeth to get a grip on.

Ceramic sleep houses are chew resistant.

Be picky, too, about the cage furniture and toys you buy—ceramic and metal accessories are gnaw proof, whereas plastic and wooden ones are not. Do you want Barney to keep a roof over his head? A ceramic sleep house will outlast a plastic one any day. Do you want Barney to have a wheel workout every day? A plastic wheel could have a limited life span, but a sheet-aluminum one will last a hamster's lifetime. (For more detailed information about wheels, see "Treadmill training, a.k.a. the hamster wheel" in Chapter 7.)

When you check the pet store shelves for toys, wooden and plastic ones are mostly what you'll find. Go ahead; buy a few. They'll keep your furball happy and, although they won't last forever, they're cheap to replace. However, if your pet is a plastic addict, if he's obsessive about chewing his plastic playthings, remove them from the cage altogether. Otherwise, swallowed plastic splinters could cause your hamster intestinal upset and digestive problems. Ceramic and wood toys are much safer choices for hamsters with a passion for plastic, although even these toys will have to be checked regularly and removed if they get too chewed to be safe.

When Barney's confined to his cage, there's a limit to the gnaw damage he can do. But when he's out of the cage for playtime (see Chapter 8) there are lots more targets for those industrious gnashers. During any out-of-the-cage playtime, supervision is a must. Never let

Check plastic products and playthings for nibble damage.

Barney out of your sight or that mini munching machine could have a field day.

Plastic cage headaches . . . and solutions

If your hamster is an incorrigible chewer, a plastic habitat could be a real headache. Although some brands of hamster homes have chew-resistant plastic in problem areas, not all do. And anyway, *chew resistant* does not mean *chew proof*. So, if your pet calls a plastic habitat home, keep your eyes peeled. On every side there are gnawable surfaces. It's your job to watch and see just where Barney launches his tooth attacks. Likely targets will be connecting tubes, the little lookout rooms on the tops of towers, maze walls, and any part of the cage itself that your hamster can get a grip on with his teeth, such as vent holes or edges. Inspect the whole cage system on a regular basis. And if you do find gnaw damage, don't wait until tomorrow to take action; it takes very little time for Barney to turn a miniscule hole into an escape hole.

What action *can* you take to discourage a determined home wrecker?

The first thing to do is make a trip to the pet store and arm yourself with a bitter deterrent product such as Bitter Apple, Bitter Lime, or Bitter End. Don't buy a spray because it evaporates quickly and won't deter Barney's gnawing for long. Buy a cream or gel, which lasts longer and can be dabbed exactly where you want it. All of these products have a very bitter taste, but none of them will harm your pet. He'll just hate the taste of the stuff (well, most hamsters will). Smear a little of the cream onto the gnaw zone. Then, when Barney next tries to nibble, he'll back off quickly and think twice about attacking the same spot again. You might have to reapply the cream/gel from time to time to reinforce the message.

Will this strategy work for all hamsters? Unfortunately, there are no guarantees. Some hamsters have oddball tastes. Your Barney might actually *like* the flavor of Bitter Apple. What then? Try another product. The unpleasant taste of the herbs in Bitter End might work when the flavor of Bitter Apple or Bitter Lime won't. What if your hamster is overwhelmed by the smell of the creams/gels? In this case, you could try an odorless spray like Fooey or Yuck!.

Have you tried more than one product and struck out each time? Then forget the deterrent tactics and go for a replacement program instead. Throw away the gnawed accessory and replace it with something that has a different design. For example, if Barney is eating through his restaurant, replace it with a tree house. The tree house might not have the same handy corner, edge, lip, or vent hole that gave Barney a tooth hold on the bistro.

Still no luck? Has the tree house suffered the same fate as the restaurant? The only option now is to minimize the use of plastic. Wherever possible, buy metal or ceramic accessories. If necessary, get rid of the plastic habitat in favor of wire or glass units. Of course, in a multimodule setup, you'll still have the plastic connecting tubes. You could minimize chew damage by buying the tubes that have metal no-chew connecting rings. But only the rings are metal—the tubes themselves are plastic. So, don't be lulled into a false sense of security . . . all connecting tubes should be checked frequently and replaced when necessary. As for

A crunchy carrot gives teeth a workout.

Chomp, chomp . . .

plastic tube toys inside the cage, get rid of them. Switch instead to Chubes Play Tubes. These are made of edible vegetable parchment; your pet can play in them and safely snack on them as well.

. . . chew, chew.

Hamster teething treats

Your hamster is going to chew. And chew. And chew. It's up to you to provide him with something owner approved to chomp on. If you stock his cage with chewables, your pet will get the gnawing he needs and he'll be less likely to attack his cage or cage furniture. Are lab blocks a part of Barney's basic diet? Good. While he's getting his nutrition, he'll be getting his teeth trimmed, too. But lab blocks aren't the only answer. You can buy lots of colorful, flavorful, inexpensive hamster chewies for Barney to exercise his teeth on. Look for hardwood chews like critter kabobs, critter cubes, hamster bites, Swiss chews, or veggie sticks. Tasty treats like nibble bars, alfalfa squares, dog biscuits, and crunchy gnaw sticks do double duty . . . they file down the fangs while appealing to the taste buds. Some hamsters take a fancy to Nylabones and cornstarch-based Booda velvet bones; others won't touch them. It's all a matter of personal taste.

But you don't need to go the store-bought route for gnawables. If the budget is tight, coconut shells or empty Brazil nut shells will give your pet's teeth a good workout. Or, have you got any trees in your backyard? Barney might appreciate some all-natural chews. Leafy twigs and branches from maple, apple, pear, aspen, oak, or willow trees are not only good to chew on, they have nutritional value, too. Just make sure that anything you offer Barney comes from trees that have never been sprayed. And, rinse the branches well to get rid of any creepy crawlies. Although twigs from the backyard are OK, wood from the home workshop is not. You can't be certain that wood picked up at the local lumberyard has never been treated with chemicals or preservatives.

A big block of wooden cheese will last longer than small chewies.

One last word on this toothy topic. Gnawing is normal, but obsessive gnawing is not. Compulsive chewing has more to do with boredom than with keeping teeth trimmed. If Barney is exercising those chompers nonstop, then perhaps he needs a more expansive cage setup, more out-of-the-cage playtime, and more stimulating toys.

Chapter Six

Potty Training

Why bother?

Ugh . . . what's that smell? It's no secret that hamster urine has a strong odor. By the end of a week, that pungent aroma wafting around your hamster's cage will be getting up your nose and on your nerves. And just think, if the offending smell has you holding your nose as you walk by, how much worse will it be for poor Humphrey who's stuck in the cage? With his acute sense of smell, he'll be gagging in no time. Even worse, the ammonia fumes produced when urine breaks down can irritate Humphrey's respiratory membranes and make him sick.

Hamster potties come in different shapes. Rectangular . . .

However, if you train your hamster to confine his waste to a covered potty that can be emptied frequently, you'll go a long way toward eliminating the fumes and the smell. You'll be happier. Your hamster will be happier. That cage will be a more comfortable and healthy place for your pet. What better reasons to give potty training a try? And there's an added bonus . . . potty training also cuts down on the time you have to spend cleaning out the cage.

Is it possible?

Okay, litter training would be a big plus for your hamster. Now the question is, can it be done? The answer, believe it or not, is YES. In most cases, hamsters take to potty training in the cage like ducks to water. Why? Because hamsters are clean animals whose natural habit is to urinate (but not always to defecate) in the same spot all the time, usually in a corner. To train your pet, you take advantage of this trait and place a hamster outhouse into the corner that he chooses as his bathroom.

The right equipment

Start by finding a suitable hamster potty. You're in luck here! Most pet shops that carry hamster supplies have potties in stock at a price that won't break the bank. Some are triangular to fit nicely into a cage corner; others are rectangular. All have hinged or removable tops and a hamster-sized opening in the front.

If you don't want to go the store-bought route, you can easily devise a homemade latrine at no cost whatsoever. First, look for a small, sturdy plastic container with a lid. Next, cut a 2- to 3-inch (5- to 7.5-cm) diameter hole in the side of the container. Locate this hole about 1 inch (2.5 cm) above the base (1/2 inch [1.3 cm] for dwarf hamsters) so that litter won't scatter when Humphrey's in there doing his business. Last, sand the edge smooth for safe entries and exits.

A homemade plastic privy might have to be replaced from time to time if the plastic absorbs the urine odor or if Humphrey shows any interest in gnawing it. Unfortunately, most plastic containers are not nibble proof. So, rather than providing Humphrey with a plastic potty, you might want to give him a nonporous, gnaw-proof, glass potty instead.

The great thing about a glass outhouse is that there are absolutely no do-it-yourself skills involved in setting one up. All you need to do is get hold of a 1-pint (500-mL), wide-mouth jar—or a 1/2-pint (250-mL) jam jar for a dwarf hamster—pop it into a corner of the cage, and there you have it, an instant hamster restroom. It's easy to clean, it's not a tooth target, and it will last as long as your hamster does. Just make sure that the toilet jar is big enough for your pet to turn around in.

. . . and triangular.

After the potty's picked, litter is next on the list. Store-bought hamster toilets come complete with a little bag of litter and a scoop. Of course, that little bag won't last long, so you should pick up a refill box when you buy the potty. If you can't find refills of the hamster litter that's packaged with the toilets, you could buy dust-free, scent-free clumping cat litter instead. The clumping clay type is economical and makes for easy cleanup . . . just scoop out the clumps daily and give the potty a good wash once a week . . . but many owners steer clear of it because it contains silica dust that

One glass jar + litter = a hamster potty

can be harmful to a pet's health. Clumping wheat is a better choice as long as you buy one of the new-and-improved dust-free varieties. And clumping corncob might be OK as long as the scent is to your hamster's liking.

Another option is to use a pelleted litter made from wood, paper, grain, or grass. On the downside, these pellets can't be scooped as easily as can the clumping litter because it's hard to distinguish soiled pellets from fresh ones. But on the plus side, the wood, grain, and grass pellets are so superabsorbent and do such a great job of odor control that they don't need to be scooped. You just toss them out every few days, then wash and refill the outhouse.

Is it possible to use your hamster's regular bedding as litter? Yes it is! After all, that's exactly what Humphrey would be using if you hadn't provided him with a potty. However, if shavings are used as bedding, you'll need to clean out the toilet on a daily basis because shavings get wet and stay wet . . . and smelly, too.

Here's an important point you must always keep in mind—make sure that your hamster doesn't eat or pouch his litter. Some litters can damage cheek pouches; others are hazardous to your hamster's health if swallowed. And even if a litter is safe to eat or pouch, your hamster shouldn't be eating it instead of food. So, if you see Humphrey snacking on grain pellets or packing his pouches with clumping corncob, get rid of that litter right away and try something else.

Getting down to business

You've chosen the potty and the litter . . . now it's Humphrey's turn to make a choice. He has to pick out the location for his lavatory. Whatever corner gets his repeat business is the corner where the potty should be placed. Don't bother making the choice yourself without consulting Humphrey. He'll just ignore you and go where *he* wants to go. Are you setting up a new cage with all the bells and whistles? Be patient. Don't put the litter box into the cage until your hamster christens a corner.

When the bathroom facilities are in place, toilet training can begin. Cover the bottom of the potty with litter, and add some urine-soaked bedding along with a few droppings. As soon as Humphrey's wide-awake, place him at the outhouse opening so that he can get a whiff of what's inside. This lets him know what that funny little house in the corner is for. Then, when nature calls, his natural instinct should take over and prompt him to step right in to relieve himself.

Never ever force your hamster into the potty. You don't want to get your fingers nipped, and you don't want to turn him off the idea of toilet training. Instead, let him investigate the litter box at his own pace. Most hamsters eventually catch on.

A difference of opinion

Some hamsters are delighted with their new bathroom . . . but not for its intended purpose. They see it as a bedroom or a kitchen and prefer to sleep there or stash food in it. What are the reasons for this? Usually, a hamster sleeps in his litter pan either because he hasn't been provided with separate sleeping quarters or because the sleep box he has been given isn't to his liking. Usually a hamster hoards food in the litter pan because the cage is too small for him to find alternative hiding places for

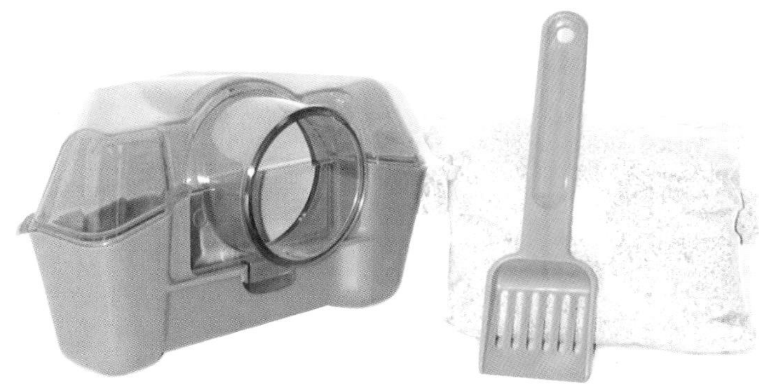

Store-bought potties come complete with litter and a scoop.

the food. What can you do to get Humphrey to use his potty as a potty?

First, take a look at the cage. Is it big enough to accommodate a litter box, exercise equipment, at least one comfy sleeping house, and still have room left over for several food stashes? If not, get a bigger cage or add more sections to the existing one. If the size of the cage isn't the problem, then take a look at Humphrey's sleep house. Is it the right size? Does he need a second one? Or, could the nesting material be unsuitable? Reread Chapter 1 to review the information on cages, beds, and bedding.

The uncooperative hamster

Hamsters aren't always 100 percent cooperative about litter training. For example, your pet might decide that it's OK to urinate in the box but not to defecate in it. This is common, and there's not much you can do to change this behavior. However, it's easy enough to get rid of the droppings between cage cleanings. Just pick them out with an old spoon or a pair of tweezers. And talking about droppings, don't get upset if you notice your furball gobbling down one or two. Hamsters practice coprophagy, which means they eat some of their soft feces to obtain residual vitamins. This isn't as gross as it sounds . . . it's just a hamster's way of recycling food to get the maximum nutritional value from it.

"I know what this box is for!"

Another way a hamster can be uncooperative is to use more than one corner for bathroom breaks, especially if he's housed in a large or multisection cage. Don't try to train him to use a single corner. This could cause him undue stress. Instead, follow his lead, and put potties into each of his chosen corners.

Although most hamsters are good candidates for litter training, there's always the odd renegade that doesn't get the hang of things. Be patient; often it's just a matter of time. However, if the box continues to be boycotted, don't force the issue. Rather than upsetting yourself and stressing your hamster, it's better to use highly absorbent bedding in the cage and resign yourself to daily corner cleaning.

Chapter Seven

Make the Cage a Hamster Heaven

Phys. ed. . . . your hamster needs a daily workout

Take a look at your small hamster with her short legs. Would you ever believe that in the wild she can cover miles in a single night? Now look at her cage. How much exercise can she get in that? Face the facts . . . your hamster is going to spend much of her life in her cage. And no matter how many tubes and modules you join together, you won't be able to give Phoebe miles of cage to explore. So what's the answer? Well, it's a combination of things. You have to give her as expansive a cage setup as possible (see Chapter 1). You have to give her as much out-of-the-cage playtime as possible (see Chapters 8 and 9). And, you have to give her toys, running wheels, climbers, and other playthings to keep her mind occupied and her little legs on the move.

The quality of Phoebe's life is totally up to you. She can't run out and pick out toys to pep up her life. It's *you* who will have to make that cage a hamster health club . . . a fitness center and playground all rolled into one. In such a stimulating environment, your hamster will be able to follow her natural instincts and get the workout she needs. She'll be able to keep her body in shape and her mind alive. In other words, she'll be happy. And a happy hamster is easy to handle and easy to train.

Run, run, run, run, run . . . run, run, run, run, run . . .

Treadmill training, a.k.a. the hamster wheel

How do you provide your pet with the marathon practice she needs? The easiest way is to let her loose on a hamster wheel. However, not all hamster wheels are created equal—you must be careful in your choice. If you buy a wheel that has rungs to run on, Phoebe's fragile feet and legs could get caught in the rungs and injured or broken. For safety's sake, your best bet is to buy a wheel with a solid running surface. It's also a good idea to look for a wheel that's open on one side and completely solid on the other. This type of wheel makes for easy entrances and exits, and it's a safe choice because there are no crossbars to get in your hamster's way. Good examples of these Phoebe-friendly wheels are Hagen Habitrail All-Terrain Wheels, Super Pet Comfort Wheels, and Transoniq Wodent Wheels. These are all plastic with solid running surfaces. So, too, are the enclosed wheels that attach to the tube openings of plastic habitats. However, before buying one of these, make sure it's big enough for your four-legged friend.

The safest wheels have a solid running surface.

Some hamsters like to exercise their teeth as well as their legs. If your pet is making a meal of her plastic wheel, you should remove it (remember, chewed plastic can play havoc with your pet's digestion) and switch to a metal wheel. This is easier said than done . . . you might have trouble finding the perfect metal wheel. Most of them have rungs. Fern Cage and Quality Cage wheels don't—they have solid running surfaces made of powder-coated sheet metal. Both brands are gnaw proof. Both come in a range of sizes and can be placed onto the cage floor or hung from the cage wires. Unfortunately, they also have those annoying crossbars.

Wheel size is all-important, too. A wheel that's too small can cause spinal damage by forcing your hamster to bow her back unnaturally as she runs. So don't buy a small hamster wheel for your baby Syrian. That baby's gonna grow, but the wheel won't. A small wheel will be fine for a dwarf hamster. But if you have more than one of these minimammals living together, you'll need to provide more than one wheel—otherwise, fights will start and the fur will fly.

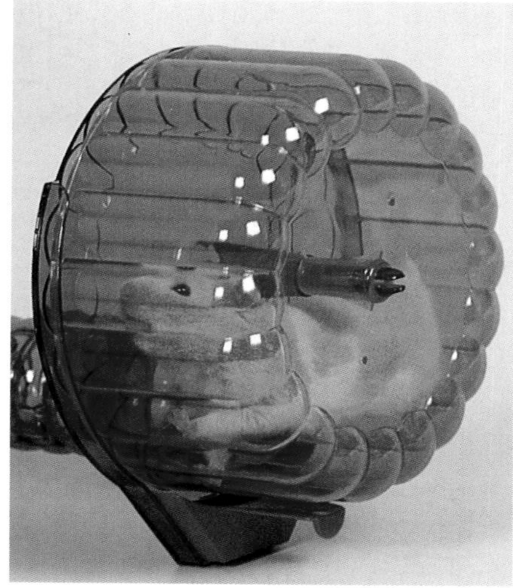

left: Most metal wheels have rungs.

right: Some wheels cater to your hamster's comfort with a removable pee and poop tray.

One of the main points to consider when you're scouting out wheels is the noise factor. Phoebe won't care how much racket she makes on her nightly marathons. But you might! Or your spouse might, or your kids might, or your neighbors might. There's nothing more annoying at 3:00 A.M. than the rumble-rumble or the squeak-squeak of a noisy hamster wheel. So spin those wheels at the pet shop before parting with your cash. Are *none* of the pet store wheels quiet? You might be able to fix a squeaky one at home with a few drops of vegetable oil. If this doesn't work, return it and surf the Net for a noiseless one.

Often a cage comes complete with a wheel . . . and often this wheel isn't the greatest. Check it out. Is it too small or does the running surface have rungs? Don't keep a substandard wheel just because it comes with the cage. For your hamster's sake, ditch it and pick another model.

Because hamsters are such big fans of wheel running, some become obsessive wheel whirlers and run to the point of exhaustion. If you find that Phoebe is jogging round and round nonstop, perhaps it's because she has nowhere else to run. Is her cage setup too small? Give her a more extensive cage layout for added running room. Does she have no other equipment to exercise on? Right from the start, a wheel should be just one exercise option among many (see the next section). Does she get enough out-of-the-cage playtime? Running free in a supervised play area should be part of her daily routine.

Sometimes a bigger cage, more equipment, and extra out-of-the-cage exercise time will make no difference to Phoebe's compulsive running. In this case, let her run the wheel in the early evening, but take it out of the cage when you go to bed at night so that she has to explore other exercise options.

Banish boredom

Phoebe's going to spend hours and hours and hours in her cage. Don't let those hours be dull, boring ones. Instead, provide your pet with many and varied activities to keep her on the move and keep the old brain cells working. Set up a network of tunnels and mazes to give Phoebe roam room in a limited space. Be sure to secure the lid of a maze to the maze itself by taping it down tightly or by securing the top to the bottom with a tight-fitting rubber band or a long shoestring. Otherwise, your hamster could pop off the lid and pop out.

To keep Phoebe on her toes and on the ball, there are all kinds of hamster toys readily available. Look for seesaws, climbers, straight ladders, arched ladders, holey logs and tubes, grass roll-a-nests and tubes, puzzle playgrounds, and burrowing

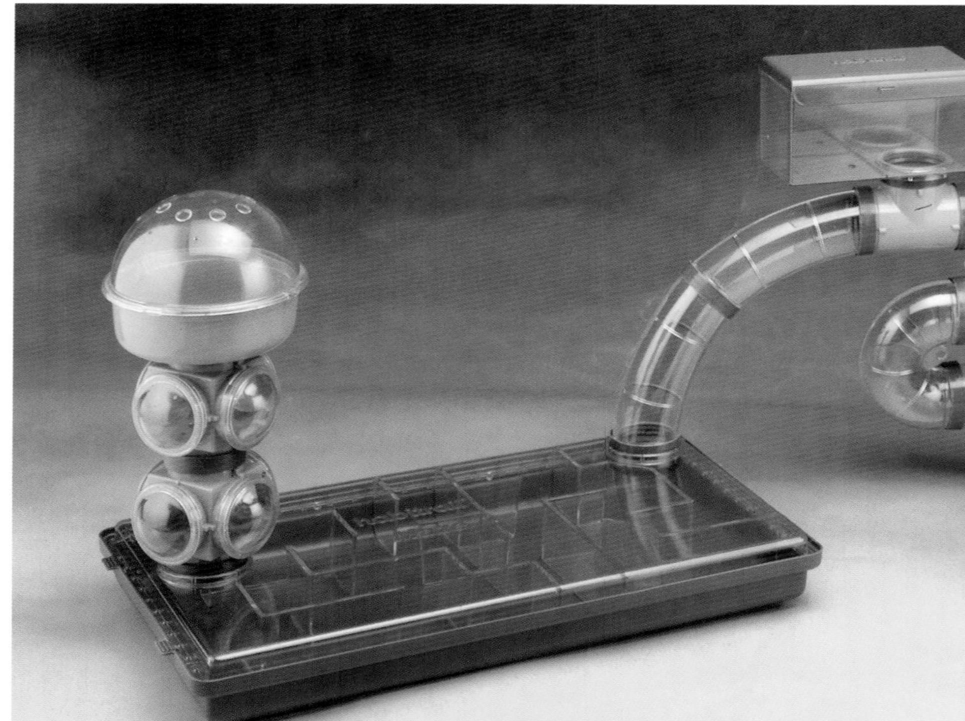

Give Phoebe her own marathon course by adding tubes and a maze to the cage setup.

boxes. These are just a few examples of store-bought hamster toys. There are lots more on the pet store shelves, with new ones coming onto the market all the time. But keep in mind that what catches your eye might not tickle Phoebe's fancy. Trial and error is the name of the game.

Is there anything around the house suitable for a hamster toy? Try paper towel or toilet paper tubes. For a dwarf hamster, they're fine as is. For a chubby Syrian, the tubes might have to be split lengthwise so she doesn't get stuck. You

Peeping out of a Puzzle Playground.

Grass toys . . .

can also crumple up some plain, unused, white paper for Phoebe to play with—computer paper, paper towels, facial tissues, or tissue paper are all OK. Cylindrical oatmeal boxes make great hamster hideaways, and sections of smooth PVC pipe make instant pet tunnels. Small clay flowerpots are also hamster favorites. Turned upside down, they're climbers; turned on their sides, they're caves.

No matter what equipment you decide to put into your pet's cage, make sure it's firmly planted on the floor of the cage. A seesaw, a ladder, or a puzzle gym that's wobbling around on lumpy bedding is an accident waiting to happen. So for safety's sake, check frequently to make sure that every toy is stable and can't topple over.

One more point . . . when setting up the cage system, plan on having several activity centers so that Phoebe is kept busy, busy, busy. The idea is to banish boredom and improve your pet's quality of life.

. . . are safe and fun.

Variety is the spice of life

One way to keep your hamster on her toes is to rearrange her cage every so often . . . one item at a time, please, so that she doesn't get stressed. For example, you could take the seesaw out of the gazebo and put it into the villa. Or, you could reconfigure the tubes that lead from the main cage to the burrowing box. Or, you could take an old toy out of the cage and replace it with a new one. To help Phoebe take to the new toy, rub it with some of her used bedding to give it that familiar fragrance. The old toy can be recycled back into the cage a few weeks later when it will seem like a new toy again.

However, don't get carried away and rearrange *everything* in the cage. Hamsters are creatures of habit . . . when it comes to their basic living arrangements, they like a place for everything and everything in its place. So don't annoy Phoebe or stress her out by moving her

Rub a new swing with old bedding to make it smell familiar.

sleep house, potty, food dish, or water bottle. Plan on moving only the fun stuff. After all, it's the fun stuff that's going to keep your hamster active and mentally alert.

Be aware, too, that some hamsters won't tolerate having even their playthings moved. These diehard stick-in-the-muds get upset and agitated by change of any kind. They like their cage contents and setup to remain the same yesterday, today, and tomorrow. So whenever you make a cage change, keep an eye on Phoebe to make sure the new arrangement is to her liking. If she becomes distressed or is unable to settle down, go back to the old, familiar arrangement.

A new toy presents a new challenge.

Chapter Eight

Out to the Playground for Recess?

Is it possible? Is it practical?

In the last chapter, you learned how important exercise is for your hamster and how to provide workout opportunities for her in the cage. But why confine exercise to the cage? One of the very best ways to see that your pet gets a good aerobic workout is to let her have some supervised out-of-the-cage roaming time. Of course, you can't let your hamster have free run of the house like a dog or a cat. Think of the safety issues. A small hamster could be stepped on and squashed; she could vanish without a trace into the walls, heating ducts, or appliances. Think, too, of the property damage she could do. You might not see *her*, but you'll certainly see the path of destruction she leaves . . . gnawed woodwork, nibbled rugs, chewed upholstery.

So, if you can't let Maude meander through the house, just how is she going to get her out-of-the-cage exercise? The answer is you can watch her run about either in a small, hamster-proofed room or in a pet playpen.

Hamster proofing

If you want to go the hamster-proofed-room route, then you have to know what hamster proofing is. In a nutshell, hamster proofing is making the hamster's play space safe—safe *for* her and safe *from* her. When you're choosing a play space, look at it first from your hamster's viewpoint. Can she escape? Can she get hurt? Then, look at it from an owner's angle. What can your pet nibble at or destroy? When you know what you have to guard against, you'll realize that the range of possible play places is fairly limited.

The best bet is the bathroom

In most homes or apartments, the bathroom is the best bet for a hamster playground. For a start, not many bathrooms are open-plan;

they usually have a door . . . better yet, a door that locks. A closed door will keep Maude in, and a locked door will keep other people out, making the bathroom a traffic-free zone. Most bathrooms are small so they won't require much hamster proofing. There's not much furniture for tooth attacks, and the floor is usually washable.

The first and easiest step in hamster proofing is to clear the decks. Pick up anything on the floor that your pet could sink her teeth into. Towels, rugs, clothes from the night before—these are chewables that should be tossed into the hallway or the laundry. And talking about towels, move any that are dangling over the side of the tub. Otherwise, when your hamster climbs aboard, towel and hamster will both come crashing down. Next, pick up any soap, shampoo, sponges, or toilet brushes that are littering the floor. And watch out for lightweight wastebaskets that could be toppled and trashed. While you're down at floor level, take a look at the heating vent covers. Fancy grillwork covers could provide an open door into the maze of the heating system. Wooden ones could get gnawed. Metal louvered types could trap, cut, or injure your pet's delicate feet. Don't take any chances. When Maude's out playing, cover up those vents. A ceramic tile makes an ideal temporary cover, but an inverted shoe box, or even a piece of heavy cardboard weighted down, will do the trick. Do you live in an older home with large, old-style heating vents? If they're on the floor, cover them up. If they're on the wall at floor level, 1/4-inch (0.6-cm) galvanized screening secured under the vents will keep out nosy, four-legged explorers. Do you have baseboard heaters rather than floor vents? Unless the design is such that Maude can't get burned and can't nibble at the wires, better plan on using a pet playpen (see the last section in this chapter).

"I'm coming! Is the hamster proofing done?"

Make sure all plugged-in electric cords are out of reach or your pet will surely try a taste . . . much to her shock. Even unplugged cords can be a hazard if they're in hamster reach. One yank on a dangling cord could bring down a curling iron onto your furball's head. Surely this is not the type of fun you had in mind for hamster playtime!

On to the plumbing now. First inspect the pipes. Can you see any gaps where the plumbing pipes come up through the floor or go into the wall? Plug up any holes with wall repair compound before your hamster vanishes from view. Even a small gap needs immediate attention because a dwarf-Maude could squeeze right in, and a gnawing Syrian-Maude could soon make a small hole into a big one.

The sink vanity is next on the bathroom checklist. Make sure it's flush against the wall. If there's a gap, your pet will see it as an escape route. Nail up a piece of wooden molding that's wide enough to cover the space. Then get down on your knees and take a close look at the kickboard under the vanity. Is there a space between kickboard and cupboard? Here's another opportunity for your hamster to crawl in and disappear. Foil her efforts. For a narrow space, nail up a piece of quarter-round molding to fill the gap. For larger openings, you'll have to remove the old kickboard.

Where can I play safely?

Then either replace it with a taller one, or cut a piece of thin plywood or wafer board to fit, nail this in place, and cover it with the old kickboard. The repair won't show unless you're lying flat on the floor!

While you're checking for spaces and gaps, scrutinize the bathroom door. It doesn't take much of a gap between door and floor for a hamster to slither under. A draft stop, a door sweep, or an old, jammed-in towel will keep Maude on the right side of the door.

Remember, hamsters love to chew. Unfortunately, you can't know in advance what your hamster's going to target. So your best plan is to wait and watch until Maude makes her move. If she goes after the kickboards or the baseboards, smear the attack zone with a bitter paste (see Chapter 5), or cover it with stick-on vinyl wall base (a.k.a. vinyl baseboard). And stay vigilant. Just because your pet didn't launch a tooth attack this week doesn't mean that she won't do so next week or six weeks down the road.

Does your indoor outhouse do double duty as a greenhouse? Watch out . . . hamsters like to dig in dirt. If yours can scramble up a flowerpot or scale a wicker planter, she'll be throwing dirt around in a flash. And what if she decides to munch on the foliage? This could be bad news because the leaves of many common household plants are poisonous to animals. Play it safe. Put all plants in the playroom out of hamster reach.

Off limits

In most homes, a bathroom makes the most practical hamster playground. However, if the bathroom's too busy in your house, there might be another room that could be used for a play place. What about a mudroom, a utility room, an exercise room, or a sewing room? As long as you can hamster proof the room, it's a possibility. Or do you have a hallway that can be closed off? That's another potential playground. Take a good look at your house. Only you can decide what area or areas can be made safe for Maude.

Are there any places that should be totally off limits? Living rooms, family rooms, and bedrooms are not usually practical playrooms. Why not? Too many places to hide, too much wood to gnaw, too much upholstery to chew, too many rugs to unravel. In other words, too much trouble. Laundry rooms aren't very practical either. Hamsters can creep under and into the washer and dryer, they can nibble the drive belts, they can climb up and fall, and they can escape to the great outdoors via a gnawed dryer vent. So, unless you can *completely* block off the appliances, keep laundry rooms off limits. Ditto with the kitchen. Other than the problem of completely hamster proofing all the appliances, there are hygiene concerns. Animals and food preparation are not a good mix . . . let Maude cook up some fun in another room.

Can you hamster proof your exercise room?

Pet playpens

Perhaps your house is too old to lend itself to hamster proofing, perhaps it's too elegant, perhaps you don't have the time. Does this mean that Maude has to languish in her cage? No! There is another option. Pet playpens to the rescue! Look for products like the Grrreat Wall or the Small Animal Playpen. These portable pet-containment systems can be set up in seconds in any room that has a washable floor. The Grrreat Wall is a roll of flexible plastic that unwinds to form a large 20-inch-high (50-cm) enclosure. The Small Animal Playpen is a colorful, vertical-wire fence that folds flat. Several can be joined together to make a larger pen.

Are you short on cash? Why not make your own pet corral? First, lay your hands on some sturdy cardboard boxes, at least 1-foot (30-cm) high. Next, remove the top and bottom flaps. Now slice right through one corner crease line on each box

No play room available? Use a pet playpen instead.

so that the cardboard can be opened out flat. Then tape the boxes together to form a pet playpen. This homemade corral has many advantages. Its size can be customized by adding or subtracting boxes, it folds flat for storage, and when it looks the worse for wear, it's a cinch to make a new one.

For an instant playpen that takes no outlay of time or money, there's always the empty bathtub. Close the drain securely, hang any shower curtain outside the tub, and cover the bottom with an old towel or blanket for a softer, less slippery walking surface. And that's all there is to it! If the bathtub's out of the question, what about a child's plastic wading pool—minus the water, of course. As long as the sides are high enough, it will give your buddy a secure place to stretch her little legs.

Warning! Whether you go the store-bought, the homemade, or the instant route, it's very important to remember that a pet playpen is NOT a baby-sitting service. Pets should NEVER be left unsupervised in a playpen.

Chapter Nine

Practice Sessions in the Play Place

Step-by-step instructions

The play place is picked out and hamster proofed. Now the question is, have you and Abe become best buddies yet? Don't introduce your hamster to the world beyond the cage until you're completely comfortable with each other. This is important. If Abe is jittery around you, leaving the security of his cage could be stressful. If you're jittery around Abe, you could drop him.

When the big moment does arrive for your pet's first out-of-the-cage adventure, make it an evening adventure. That's when, in their natural habitat, hamsters come out of their burrows to forage; that's when they're wide-awake and ready for action. Don't just plop Abe into the wide-open spaces without providing him with a burrow or bolt hole. He needs a place to run to in order to feel safe. The burrow could be either a module of his own cage system or a small travel cage customized to smell like home with used nesting material, a potty, food, and a water bottle. A door or a tube hole at or near floor level is a must for easy exits and entries.

Put Abe into the smaller safe house, carry it to the playground room or put it into the playpen, open the cage door, then sit down quietly and wait. In his own good time, Abe will amble out to investigate. Sit tight, and watch. Don't go grabbing at him, putting him here, putting him there, trying to make him play with toys. Let him check things out for himself. What you can do, however, is give your mini-Magellan a taste of the wild by setting out some treats and nesting material that he can forage for. This gives a point to his explorations and mimics what he'd do in a natural setting.

In the beginning, keep out-of-the-cage time short—perhaps ten minutes—but provide it daily so that your hamster gets used to it. When he's obviously enjoying himself, gradually stretch out that playtime period until you've worked up to an hour or so of free roaming . . . or whatever you and your hamster are comfortable with.

A small cage makes a good safe house in the play place.

Never make loud noises or sudden movements when Abe's out playing, and keep the kids under control . . . don't let them chase at, grab at, poke at, or yell at their little Livingston. After all, stressing out Abe isn't the goal of playtime.

Supervision is a must

When Abe is out, supervision is in. NEVER let your hamster run around unsupervised. No matter how sure you are about your hamster-proofing skills, there's no telling what Abe could get into or chew through when your back's turned. Do you want to come back to the bathroom and find a pile of sawdust right beside a hole in the cupboard kickboard? Of course not! So if the doorbell rings, don't leave Abe to his own devices. Pick him up and pop him back into the cage.

Do's and don'ts

Every kid on the block knows that the playground has rules, and Abe's playground should be no exception. The following do's and don'ts will help keep your hamster safe and stress free.

• *Do* let your pet out to play in the evening when he's awake and alert. Remember, waking a hamster causes it stress.

• *Do* exercise crowd control. With too many people in the play area, an accident's more likely to happen.

• *Do* keep the bathroom door locked to prevent people from barging in on playtime. You don't want

"I'm a cutie, but don't let me out to play unsupervised."

your pet getting smacked by the door or making a fast getaway.

• *Do* get into the habit of sitting down during playtime. When you're not standing up, you can't stand on Abe.

• *Don't* wear shoes . . . go around in stocking feet doing the "soft-shoe shuffle." This means sliding your feet across the floor rather than stepping normally. After all, you can't step on Abe if you don't take any steps.

• *Don't* treat Abe as a toy. He's a living, breathing creature, not a stuffed animal to be tossed around when your kids have company.

Clean up the accidents

Will your intrepid explorer use that potty you so thoughtfully provided in the "safe-house" cage? Maybe yes, maybe no. You might increase the chances of a potty break in the proper place by providing an extra potty in the room or playpen. But, even in the best-regulated households, accidents can happen. Fortunately, hamsters don't make much of a mess even when they miss. And if you've chosen the playground wisely, the floor will be easy to clean. Just wipe up any accidents with a paper towel, and give the floor a quick mop with a pet deodorizer when the fun and games are finished.

Catching that hamster

Playtime's over. It's time for Abe to go back into his cage. But Abe

When play-time's over, put treats on your palm . . .

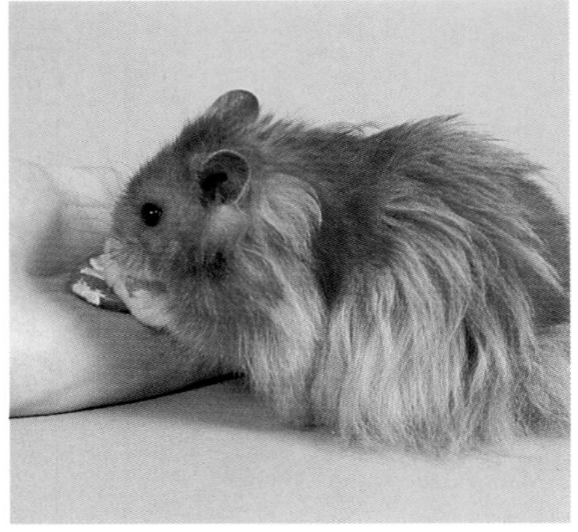

doesn't want to go back into his cage. In fact, he has no intention of going back into that cage. Now what? Whatever you do, don't chase the little renegade—you'll only frighten him. You could wait and let him wander into the cage of his own accord. But it might be a long wait. You don't have oodles of time? Try calling your pet using the knock, click, or whistle technique you learned in Chapter 4. Or, put a favorite treat onto the palm of your hand. When Abe boards your hand to get it, cup your other hand around him and cart him off to the cage.

He's not cooperating? Put some sunflower seeds into a glass jar, and when he trots in to investigate, you've got him! Pick him up, jar and all, and return him to the cage.

. . . or into a glass jar to lure your pet to you.

Chapter Ten
Leash Walking

Really?

A hamster on a leash? Is this such a far-fetched idea? Well, it is for dwarf hamsters. They're too small and squirmy to be harnessed up. But it's a different story for Syrian hamsters. Many Syrians take quite readily to leash walking. You'll even find harnesses and leashes designed just for them on the pet store shelves.

Why would you want to leash walk your hamster? If you don't have time for hamster proofing, if you don't have a suitable room for hamster playtime, if your furniture is too fancy, or if the old back and knees aren't what they used to be, leash walking could be a good way for Pippi to get some indoor exercise.

Invest in a hamster harness

You'll give the idea a try? Then before getting down to business, you'll need to go harness hunting. A collar won't do. Your pet could slip out of it if it's too loose or choke if it's too tight. And forget the ferret, guinea pig, or kitten harnesses. They're too big and not designed with a hamster in mind. What you're looking for is a small, lightweight, hamster-specific harness; most of them come with a leash attached. And try to find one that fastens with a clasp rather than a buckle. It's much easier to fit on a fast, fidgety hamster.

Don't try to harness up your pet until you and Pippi are buddy-buddy. After all, being strapped up is a new experience for her. If you rush her into it, you could be bitten. (Tip: A treat will keep her busy while you're fastening the straps.) Fit the harness carefully—too loose and she'll escape, too tight and she'll strangle. You should just be able to squeeze the tip of your baby finger under the strap. Be particularly careful when harnessing up a Teddy Bear or Angora hamster. With these fuzzballs, you need to fit to the body, not to the fur. To make sure you've got the fit right, let Pippi take her first tentative steps in an enclosed area. Then if she wriggles loose, she won't vanish altogether.

Launching into leash walking

What spot in your house will make a good walking track? Think hall, mudroom, bathroom, or any uncarpeted room that can be closed off in case of escape.

Now for some leash-walking tips. Always walk your pet in the evening when she's more likely to cooperate, and let her walk where she wants. She can't be trained to walk, sit, or heel on command like a dog. Guide her gently without yanking on the leash or lifting her off the floor . . . you don't want to hurt her. And never leave a leashed Pippi tied up to a doorknob, or she might chew through the leash and vamoose.

Start with short walks. A few minutes at a time are enough until Pippi gets the hang of things. Then gradually increase the time spent leash walking until she's getting a good workout each day.

When leash walking, let your pet set the pace.

Never force your hamster either into a harness or into leash walking. Some hamsters want nothing to do with the whole idea. If your pet gives leash walking the thumbs-down, better forget the notion altogether and go to a playpen.

Is a hamster safe outdoors?

When Pippi gets used to the leash indoors, is it safe to take her leash walking outside? In a nutshell, no, not even in a fenced-in backyard. Why? Harnesses are not 100 percent escape proof, wooden fences usually have gaps under them, a chain-link fence is no fence at all to a hamster, and in most neighborhoods, there are roaming cats and predatory birds on the lookout for a tasty morsel.

Is there any way, then, that a hamster can get a breath of fresh air? Here's an idea. On a quiet, mild, still evening, how about taking your hamster's cage out to the deck, patio, or balcony? There, you and Pippi can relax together . . . you in a lounge chair and Pippi in her cage. DO NOT under any circumstances take her out of the cage or leave her alone without supervision. Accidents can happen, weather can change quickly, and hamsters are escape artists. Your aim is not to give her outdoor freedom, it's just to let her enjoy a whiff of fresh air.

Chapter Eleven

Roll-Around Balls

An easy answer to the exercise question

Are your fingers all thumbs when it comes to harnessing up that hamster? Is your house impossible to hamster proof? Does your pet need more roam room than a playpen can provide? A hamster ball just might solve the problem of how your pet is going to get a good workout.

Rodent on a roll

By now you know that to stay healthy, hamsters need exercise . . . and plenty of it! You also know that they can become compulsive wheel runners if their aerobic options are limited. So your goal should be to provide different types of exercise for your pet so he doesn't get obsessed with any one activity. A roll-around ball is one exercise option that many hamsters enjoy.

These balls come in several different styles. Most common are the everyday, free-roll balls, but you'll also find some that roll on a track, some that come with stands, and others that look like race cars. They come in different sizes, too, and it's very important to pick a size that suits your pet. Miniballs are strictly for dwarf hamsters. Never put your Syrian/Golden/Teddy Bear into one of these; he won't have enough air to breathe and his back will be bent unnaturally. Never put a dwarf hamster into a large ball; as the ball turns, the dwarf hamster will be thrown around inside. If you have several brands to choose from at the store, opt for the one that has plenty of ventilation holes.

How does a roll-around ball work? You put Scooter inside the hollow plastic sphere, close the door securely, and when your pet starts running, the ball starts rolling. Most hamsters enjoy taking a whirl in a ball. And some hamsters become such expert navigators that they can maneuver it exactly where they want it to go. Why not set up a miniature obstacle course if you have one of these skillful drivers?

One of the great advantages of this exercise equipment is that your

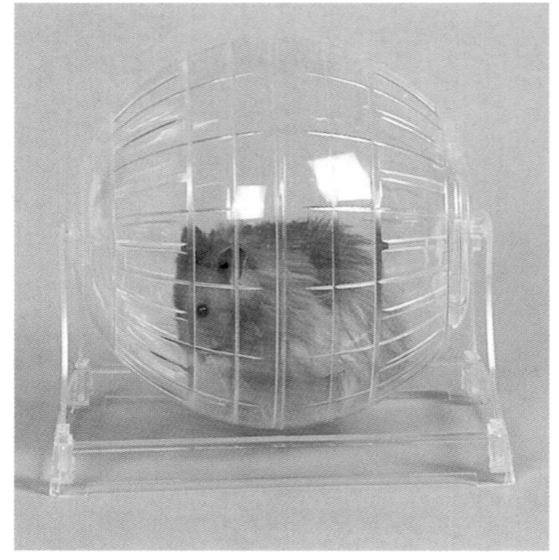

This ball is dual purpose. It can roll free on the floor or double as a wheel when put on its stand.

pet's playtime won't be limited to a small room any longer. He'll be able to expand his horizons and explore non-hamster-proofed rooms, all in the safety of an enclosed plastic sphere. But if you don't want your fuzzy friend rolling around the house at will, why not invest in a Hamster Trac? A Scooter rolling on a track will be able to rack up the miles without rolling out of sight.

Zooming around in a hamster mobile.

"Gimme a break"

No matter how much Scooter enjoys touring around the house or track in his own hamster mobile, don't let him ride to the point of exhaustion—too much running and he could dehydrate. Keep in mind, too, that a hamster can always get out of an exercise wheel when he needs a drink or a rest, but he's stuck in that ball until you let him out. So the onus is on you to monitor his ball rolling and to make sure that the kids never pop him in and forget him.

Caution—hamster at play!

To make sure your hamster can exercise safely, here are the roll-around rules.

- After putting your hamster into the ball, latch the door properly to prevent escape or injury.
- Keep the ball on the floor. Never let Scooter roll it on a raised surface like a table. Even a short fall could have fatal consequences.
- Block off any steps or stairs that the ball could bounce down.
- Keep other pets well away from Scooter in his roll-a-ball. A wily ferret could open the door; a cat or dog could bat the ball around and frighten or hurt the hamster.
- Never let anyone push or kick-start the hamster roadster. Scooter's the one who has to get the ball rolling.
- Supervise, supervise, supervise.

left: "What? You want me in there?"

right: "OK! Let's give it a try!"

Not a hit with your hamster?

When you introduce your pet to this exercise activity, stick to the tried-and-true training techniques . . . start with short sessions and work up to longer ones. Take your cue from Scooter. If he's obviously enjoying himself, it's all systems go. If he seems frightened or doesn't want to get into the ball, forget the whole idea. It's not worth having a stressed-out hamster.

Wendy always supervises when her hamster is rolling around in the ball.

Chapter Twelve
Fun Time

Off to the store

Want to keep your pet on her toes? Want to make sure she's never bored? Want to create—even in a small way—the opportunities for physical and mental stimulation that wild hamsters get on their nightly foraging expeditions? Then fun activities, both in the cage and in the play area, are a must for your pet.

Head down to the pet store, and check out the hamster aisle for a wide variety of toys and fun stuff. You'll find holey wooden shapes for Goldie to climb in and out of, grass and bamboo balls and grass tunnels for her to hide in and chew, as well as colorful cars, shoes, trucks, and airplanes that she can climb on and crawl through. Now the question is, with so much choice, how do you know what will appeal to your hamster? Will Goldie go for the ladder or the Swing O' Fun, the puzzle cube or the grass getaway, the rocket or the airplane? Unfortunately, you can't tell in advance which items will get her vote and which ones she'll veto. But fortunately, hamster toys aren't usually expensive, so a snubbed toy won't be a major financial blow.

Goldie likes variety in her life and will lose interest in a toy that she's explored a hundred times already. Even the best playthings become boring with overuse. So introduce new toys on a regular basis, remove familiar toys and reintroduce them at a later date, or combine and recombine old toys in new ways . . . anything to keep the environment novel and challenging.

And, remember, always check play stuff regularly for wear and tear. Throw out anything that's too chewed up to be safe.

Round and round the wheel goes

The first thing you're going to notice on the pet store shelves is the most basic item of hamster hardware, the exercise wheel. Nearly all hamsters take to the wheel like ducks to water—no training needed here. Look back to "Treadmill training, a.k.a. the hamster wheel" in Chapter 7 for help in choosing a suitable wheel and important information on its use and potential abuse.

Will your hamster like a grass hut or a bamboo ball?

Tubes and tunnels

You can never provide too many tubes and tunnels for your hamster. After all, in the wild, hamsters spend their days hiding and sleeping in a network of underground tunnels. So if you don't have a cage system with interconnecting tubes, it's a good idea to set up a trail system in the play area. Connect straight or curved plastic hamster tubes to elbows, U-turns, tee's, and six-way cubes for a challenging labyrinth. Fortunately, you don't have to spring for everything at once . . . you can build it up a piece at a time. And to keep Goldie interested, you can recombine the sections into new configurations every so often.

Here's a unique type of tunnel system that will challenge the imagination of hamster lovers young and old. It's the CritterTrail Puzzle Playground, a system of snap-fit plastic pieces that can be joined together in endless combinations that your furry friend can explore. Putting together the frames, clear plates, passageways, rings, tubes, and slides can provide an afternoon of family fun. (Hint: the pieces are a lot easier to assemble on a hard surface, such as a kitchen table.) The Puzzle Playground can be

Would your pet prefer a school bus or a taxi ride?

used inside the cage or out in the play area.

Up, up, up

Hamsters have got strong legs for their small size. This muscular strength makes them natural climbers. So give yours something to climb on. A trip to the pet shop will turn up small wooden bird ladders, puzzle cubes, low-level bird gyms, hamster play parks, and Gym-Bar wire ladders, arches, monkey bars, and twist tunnels. Or, you can provide tree branches for free. See "Hamster teething treats" in Chapter 5 for a list of good tree choices. However, if the branches from your own backyard aren't bug free, pesticide free, and fungicide free, or if they've been polluted with exhaust fumes or road salt, then buy untreated ones at the pet shop.

What goes up, must come down—and in a hamster's case, it's often with a thump. Although Goldie is surefooted on the way up, she's not that coordinated when it comes to getting down. In fact, a hamster will often intentionally drop from a height rather than climb down. This isn't too much of a problem in a wild hamster's natural habitat where a falling hamster would have a soft, sandy landing. But if your mountaineering pet goes into a free fall in her cage or play area, she's liable to have a serious crash landing. A broken leg, pelvis, or spine is not uncommon for hamsters that fall, even from modest heights. So the number one rule when picking climbing apparatus for Goldie is keep the climbers low. A hamster that can't get up high can't come down splat!

If your hamster does fall from a height and shows any signs of limping, dragging, hiding, or acting oddly, don't take a wait-and-see attitude. Please take her to a veterinarian immediately in case she has suffered an injury.

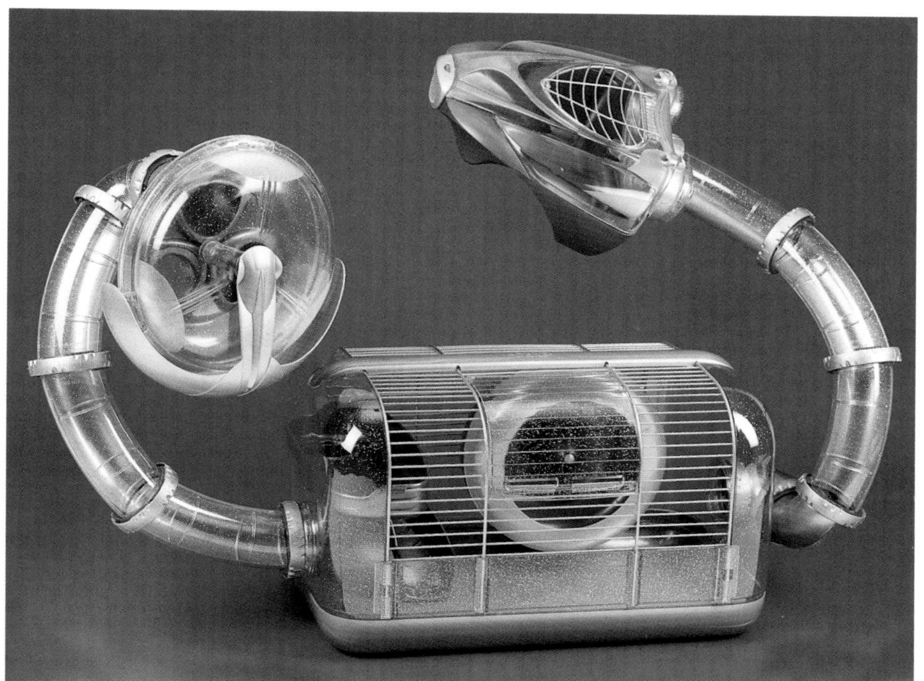

Wheels can be set up inside or outside the cage.

Down, down, down

Hamsters are not only agile climbers, they're also adept diggers. So here's an opportunity to provide your pet with a toy she'll really enjoy. Buy a burrowing module for the cage setup. Either invest in a unit made for the purpose, such as the S.A.M. Tunnel-Vue, or buy a small add-on cage module that can be turned into a digging tank. Then, for your pet's burrowing fun, fill the new unit with soft bedding, like aspen shavings or CareFRESH.

In the play area, why not give Goldie her own sandbox? Buy a cheap, plastic, extra-deep dish pan or storage box and a bag of play sand. Pour the sand into the box until it's about half full. Pop in your pet, and let her dig to her heart's content. Some buried sunflower seeds or yogurt drops will turn the digging expedition into a treasure hunt.

Teeter-totter training

Most hamsters are big teeter-totter fans, whether they're going up and down on a wire or wooden seesaw or inside the plastic-tube kind (see photos). Of course, this is a solo activity for your pet . . . there won't be a hamster at each end. What a hamster does is run up one side of the seesaw and down the other . . . again and again and again. Some hamsters catch on to this pastime without help. But if your Goldie's not the smartest hamster on the block or on the teeter-totter, here's what to do. Take small pieces of her favorite treat and line them up the middle of the seesaw. Dabs of Nutri-Cal or Toob Snax will help glue them in place. Then as Goldie walks up the seesaw to get the treats, her weight will tip the balance, and she'll get the feel of how the teeter-totter works. Repeat the treat line daily until Goldie uses the toy without a treat reward.

Homemade toys

Making homemade hamster toys is a great way to keep the kids busy on a rainy Saturday afternoon. For

Up, up, up!

Down, down, down!

Teeter-totter or seesaw? It's all the same to me . . .

. . . FUN!

A challenging playground keeps your pet on the ball.

starters, how about a pet play box? All that's needed is a small, sturdy cardboard box and a pair of scissors. Cut out a few hamster-sized holes in the box, and there you have it—an almost instant Goldie box. To make a bunker instead, cut two holes in the top of the box and bury the box in the cage bedding so that only the holes are visible. Now your pet has a bolt hole when she wants to hide.

Mazes are another hamster favorite. Get the kids to put one together from wrapping paper tubes, shoe boxes, plastic pretzel jars, cereal boxes, short lengths of PVC tubing, and cylindrical oatmeal containers. This will be a fun project for the kids, and the finished project will be a brainteaser for Goldie. Put it into the play area or playpen, and watch that Goldie go!

Chapter Thirteen

The Traveling Hamster

Keep hamster travel to a minimum

Hamsters are creatures of habit—they don't usually take to globe-trotting. The unfamiliar sights and sounds of travel can raise your pet's stress level. And remember, a stressed hamster can quickly become an ill hamster. So it's better not to take your hamster out of the house if you can help it. However, sometimes you won't have a choice. Got a sick hamster? Not many veterinarians make house calls. Been transferred to a new job on the other side of the country? You can't fax Buddy to his new home. For those times when a trip can't be avoided, here are some tips to make the journey as hamster friendly as possible.

Short car trips

A short car trip or taxi ride is probably going to be the extent of most hamster travel. A quick jaunt like this isn't a major undertaking. Pop Buddy into the small travel carrier from his playroom (see Chapter 9), making sure that there's some Buddy-scented bedding in it so that he feels safe. Or, stick him into a module from his cage setup, plugging up any openings with the special end caps made for the purpose. Whatever he travels in, make sure he has a place to hide. His favorite sleep house or a bunker box will do nicely.

For a short trip, Buddy won't really need food or water. But why not put in a small piece of melon or cucumber so he'll have something juicy and thirst quenching to munch on? A hidden treat or a gnaw stick will help keep his jaws busy and his mind off the journey.

Before putting your pet into the car, stick your nose out the door. Is there a chill in the air? Then preheat the car. Is the weather hot? Then cool the car down. (See the "Temperature warnings" section in this chapter.)

For the ride itself, if you don't have a passenger to hold the cage, it's a good idea to place it on the floor between the back and front seats. This way, if you have to make a sudden stop, the cage won't fly off the seat, and Buddy won't be shaken up.

Do you know the ABC's of hamster travel?

Long car trips

Suppose you have to move from Maryland to Montana and you're crossing the country by car. Looks like Buddy's going to be racking up the road miles. To get him through the trip with minimum hassle, check out the following hamster travel advice.

I'm traveling first class with a cozy sleep sack in my cage.

On a long trip, Buddy needs roam room. So forget the small travel carrier, and use one of his larger cage modules instead. A wire one is better for air circulation but leaves the seats open to tooth attacks. To prevent this, slot a sheet of thick cardboard between the cage and the car's upholstery; a collapsed cardboard box works well. A plastic module prevents gnaw attacks but can become an oven in direct sunlight. Keep an eye on the cage, and move it to the shady side of the car as needed. Sunshades made for car windows are a big help, too. They can be rolled up or down and moved from window to window, depending on the direction of the Sun's rays.

Stock the cage with all the comforts of home—fresh food, toys, chew sticks, and bedding scented with that familiar *Bouquet de Buddy*. Don't leave the water bottle in the cage, however. It could leak. Even worse, Buddy could break a tooth if he's sipping when the car hits a bump or pothole. The best way to take care of your pet's thirst when traveling is to put a couple of chunks of a watery fruit or vegetable, such as watermelon or cucumber, into the cage. Then, when you pull into a rest stop, put Buddy's bottle back into the cage while the car's parked.

The most important rule of the road is never get a traveling hamster out of his cage. Hamsters are known for quick getaways . . . and think of the havoc in the car with a hamster on the loose. Avoid this potentially dangerous situation by confining

Nibbling on a treat keeps my mind off the trip.

Buddy to his cage when the wheels are in motion.

Most people drive long distances in the daytime, just when hamsters need their rest. So, be considerate. No loud music. No screaming at the kids. No fights in the back seat. Your pet needs peace and quiet for his daytime beauty sleep.

If your travel plans involve overnight stays, Buddy needs to be in the hotel with you, not out in the car by himself. Best call ahead and reserve rooms in hamster friendly hotels. You probably won't have too much trouble finding places that will roll out the welcome mat for your pet. After all, a hamster doesn't bark, squawk, chirp, or meow. He won't disturb the other guests . . . as long as you take that noisy wheel out of his cage at night.

And talking about nighttime, remember your hamster is a night owl. He'll be lively and alert in the early hours just when you're trying to get some shut-eye. So, consign Buddy to the bathroom, and shut the door in case his overnight rustlings disturb your dreams.

Temperature warnings

When you take to the road with your hamster, always keep an eye on the weather and protect him accordingly. For example, heat can be life threatening to a hamster. It doesn't take much time in an overheated environment for your pet to become a victim of heatstroke. Even on an overcast day, all that glass in a car can create a greenhouse effect, making the car an oven. So whenever the weather's hot outside, it's important to keep the car cool inside. But what if you don't have

Familiar nesting material makes the travel cage feel like home.

air-conditioning and Buddy needs to visit the vet? The best plan is to call a cab or a friend with an air-conditioned car. Not possible? Then you'll have to figure out a way to cool down your own car for the ride. First, roll down the windows to let out excess heat. Next, raid the freezer for ice packs; you need the hard-sided kind, not the gnawable, soft-sided gel packs. If you don't have any, improvise . . . fill some glass jars with ice cubes. Now wrap the cold packs in old towels, and place them in and around the cage to create a cool microclimate for your hamster's comfort. And don't forget to take along a cooler stocked with extra freezer packs or ice cubes for the drive home.

Cold can cause problems for your pet as well. Your hamster is used to a comfortable, household environment. Although he wears a fur coat, he'll shiver and shake (and could even get pneumonia) if you stick him into an SUV that's been parked outside in subzero temperatures. Warm up your vehicle before Buddy takes a ride in it, and have something handy to throw over his cage at either end of the journey . . . something warm, waterproof, or windproof, depending on the weather.

Flying the friendly skies

You're not driving all the way out to Montana? You're taking a plane instead? What about Buddy? You can't send him by Priority Mail! But if you plan things carefully, he could fly with you. Here's what to do.

Start by contacting several airlines. Ask if they allow pets onboard . . . and will that be in the cabin with you or in pet cargo? Go with the airline that allows Buddy to travel in a cage at your feet where you can keep an eye on him. Pet cargo is too nerve-racking for a hamster. Not only is it noisy, other pet passengers can be scary. (Woof! Woof!) And, it's not just the flight that could be upsetting . . . getting to and from the plane could be stressful, too. What if it's boiling hot or freezing cold on the runway? What if the fueling truck or the baggage train rumbles past? What if a roaring jet takes off or lands nearby? Buddy could have a heart attack on the spot! So forget pet cargo—for a hamster, cabin class is the way to go.

Airlines may require you to have an approved carrier for your pet and perhaps even a pet medical certificate. Get the specific guidelines ahead of time. Get them in writing, and make sure you follow them to the letter. Keep all information with your ticket and present it at check-in. Having everything in order will avoid any last-minute surprises.

The homebody hamster

When vacation time rolls around, most people like a change of scene. Hamsters, on the other hand, prefer their regular routine . . . for them, a trip away from home can be quite unnerving. So don't plan on taking your hamster along on your vacation travels—look into pet-sitting arrangements instead. If it's just a weekend that's in question, why not let Buddy pet sit himself? Stock his cage with plenty of nonperishable food, a few treats, and an extra sipper bottle (a lone bottle could leak or get chewed). Then leave him to fend for himself for a day or two. He'll be fine as long as he's in good health and living in an escape-proof cage. But just in case of an unexpected emergency, why not leave a key with a neighbor? After all, if there's a power outage, your hamster could roast without air-conditioning or freeze without heat.

Are you planning to be gone for longer than a weekend? It's time to call in a favor and enlist a friend, relative, or neighbor to look in on Buddy . . . preferably at your house and preferably in the evening when he's up and about. The point is to keep Buddy's daily routine as normal as possible. *You* don't disrupt your pet's sleep by changing his food, water, and bedding in the daytime—neither should your pet sitter.

If it's not convenient for that obliging friend or relative to visit your house on a daily basis, maybe he/she could take Buddy in as a guest. An away-from-home stay isn't the best pet-sitting solution for a hamster because hamsters don't relish change, but you can ease Buddy's apprehension by taking along his whole cage setup or as much of it as your pet sitter has space for. Also take along a baggie of Buddy's used bedding. The sitter should rub his/her hands in the bedding before reaching into the cage to change food and water. Instead of smelling a stranger, Buddy will smell his familiar bedding and he won't be so scared.

Hanging out at home.

Look for a boarding facility that's hamster friendly.

When you're new to a neighborhood or you don't want to impose on a friend or relative, a professional pet sitter could be the answer. Let your fingers do the walking through the Yellow Pages, or check the ads in your local paper. This will add bucks to your vacation budget, but, hey—isn't Buddy worth it?

Whether your hamster is having a home stay or an away stay, give the sitter a detailed list of care instructions. Include food requirements, your veterinarian's phone number, the after-hours emergency clinic's phone number, and your vacation phone number. Be sure to tell your sitter what steps to take in the case of a medical emergency. Don't beat around the bush; spell out exactly how much you can afford for emergency veterinary care. If the estimated costs are going to be higher, ask the sitter to call you for instructions.

It's not usually a good idea to take a hamster to a pet-boarding facility such as a kennel, a pet store, or a veterinary clinic. Barking, screeching, yowling, clanging doors, ringing phones, overbright lights, and unfamiliar smells could give your hamster the jitters. Avoid any facility that can't guarantee that your hamster will be kept by itself in a quiet location. And, remember, seeing is believing. Check out the place for yourself—don't take someone else's word for it.

Chapter Fourteen

Handy Hints

Hamsters and other pets

Are you feeling sorry for your single hamster, all alone in that big cage? Do you think she needs a friend? Think again. Hamsters LIKE being alone. Although some dwarf hamsters get along with one or two of their own kind, Syrian hamsters are strict loners. They don't get along with other hamsters, and they rarely get along with other pets. So forget the matchmaking. You won't make your hamster happy, and introductions to other pets could end in disaster.

Outside the cage, any large pet could pounce on and harm a small hamster in the blink of an eye. Even inside the cage, Henrietta's not as safe as you might think. Although she's not at risk of bodily harm, she could well be at risk from stress. After all, a dog barking at the door of her cage could have her jumping out of her skin. A cat clambering over her cage could give her conniption fits. So keep Henrietta and her cage in a room where other pets can't prowl around and terrorize her.

How about Reggie Rat or Gerry Gerbil? They're about the same size as Henrietta. Would they make cool companions? Forget it. Hamsters are territorial, and they're no fonder of other small animals than they are of other hamsters. If you introduce your hamster to another small pet, fist fights or duels to the death are inevitable.

Taking medication

Henrietta's under the weather. You have medication for her from the veterinarian. Now the question is, how do you get the medication into that sick furball? With some flavored stuff, you won't have a problem . . . your pet will lap it right up. But with other medicines, she'll turn up her nose and clamp her jaws shut. Can you get her to swallow it? You can if you've got a spoonful of sugar to make the medicine go down. Well, maybe not . . . but a tasty mealworm coated with medicine might do the trick. You're not a fan of live treats? Try mixing the medicine into some yogurt, Nutri-Cal, or Toob Snax (see

Hamsters and other rodent pets don't mix.

Chapter 4). In most cases, your hamster will fall for the con. If not, contact your vet.

Here's a medical alert. Never treat your hamster with homemade remedies, and never give your hamster medications that haven't been prescribed by a veterinarian. You could kill her rather than cure her.

Grooming

The good news about grooming is that hamsters take care of this chore themselves. In fact, grooming is a big part of a happy and contented hamster's daily routine. She'll lick her paws, comb her fur, wash her face—over and over and over again. And again. You might give a hand to a longhaired or Angora hamster when bedding gets stuck in her fur. But even then, it's just a matter of a quick brush with a soft-bristled toothbrush. As for baths, scrub the thought—hamsters don't need 'em. Their furry little bodies take a long time to dry, and bathing puts them at risk of catching cold.

There's no need to clean Henrietta's ears, brush her teeth, or clip her claws. She can look after her ears herself. You help her to keep her teeth clean and trimmed to the right length by supplying her with chew toys—gnawing is nature's answer to dental care. The miles that she racks up racing on the wheel, scurrying through tunnels, and exercising in the play area wear down her claws—running is nature's answer to a pedicure.

It's not very common, but now and again a hamster's incisors or claws can get too long. What should you do? Take your pet to the veterinarian . . . tooth trimming and claw clipping are not jobs for an owner to tackle.

Cage-cleaning tips

You might be off the hook for hamster grooming, but you're certainly not off the hook for cage cleaning. This is the biggest chore for hamster owners, especially if Henrietta's living quarters include an extensive tunnel system. Unfortunately, there are no self-cleaning hamster habitats on the market yet! Where do you start?

Begin with the bathroom area(s). Remove the soiled bedding daily, wipe out the corner(s), and put fresh bedding down. If your hamster uses a potty, scoop the clumps daily, and wash out the potty once a week.

While you're taking care of daily corner cleanup, check for stashed food, too. Look in every nook and cranny, under bedding, in hideaways, and behind sleep houses. Hamsters often cache some of their food, saving it for a rainy day. If you're not vigilant, stashed food can soon become spoiled food. You don't want Henrietta feasting on moldy snacks.

Roughly once a week, you'll have to spring-clean the whole cage setup. Depending on how big the cage system is, this can be a time-consuming chore, so your hamster will have to cool her heels in a travel cage while you get down to cleaning. First take out all toys, wheels, sipper bottles, and bowls. Wash them with hot water and unscented soap, and rinse very well. Don't use strong-smelling soap or disinfectants that could bother Henrietta—remember she has a very keen sense of smell. Next, remove and toss out the bedding from the cage modules. Scrub and rinse each one thoroughly. Now it's on to the tubes—a Toob-A-Brush or a bottlebrush is a handy-dandy tool here. When the whole setup is squeaky clean, dry each piece inside and out, put in fresh bedding, and reassemble the habitat.

Sleep houses—and anywhere else your hamster lays her head—require special treatment. After washing and rinsing, put back some of the used bedding material along with the fresh stuff. This way, the

Hamsters are self-grooming . . . no baths needed.

Cleaning tubes is a real chore. A bottlebrush makes the job easier.

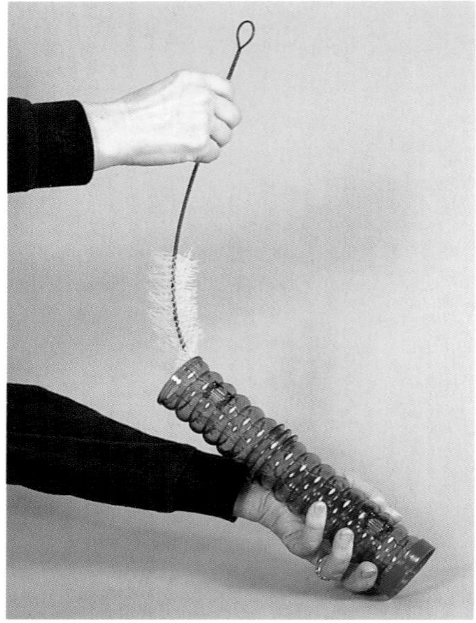

sleeping areas smell familiar to Henrietta's twitching nose.

Don't neglect the weekly cleaning ritual . . . it's one of your most important tasks if you want to keep your hamster healthy and happy. A hamster *likes* a clean habitat, and she depends on you to keep it that way.

Run, run, run, run, runaway

Whoosh! What was that scooting by? Is there a mouse in the house? Did a dust bunny fly past? No! It's your gold-medal hamster sprinter on the loose again. Don't be fooled by that chunky body and ungainly waddle . . . a runaway hamster can move fast and evade capture. If Henrietta manages to chew her way out of her habitat, or push up the lid of her sky restaurant, or hightail it out of an open door, she could vanish without a trace in minutes. Then how are you going to track her down?

First, narrow the search by figuring out which room she's in. How? Get out some sunflower seeds, and lay a little pile of ten seeds on the floor of each room in the house or apartment. Close the doors to every room, and stuff any gap between door and floor with rolled-up towels. The next morning, do the rounds and check for missing seeds—an escaped hamster is bound to get hungry sooner or later. The room with the missing seeds is the room with the missing hamster.

Now that you know where she is, how do you capture the escapee? In fact, how do you even find her? Henrietta could be holed up anywhere . . . under the furniture, in the plants, behind the books in the bookcase, inside the sofa bed. Get the picture? Check the obvious hidey-holes. No luck? Try putting her cage in the room at floor level. The scent of home sweet home might be enough to lure her in. Chances are you'll soon find her snoozing soundly in her sleep house. If you don't, it's time to set a trap. Many books and Internet sites recommend putting a ramp up to a bucket and baiting both with seeds or raisins. The idea is to entice the hamster up the ramp and into the bucket. Once in, the captured pet can't get out again. The problem is, a hamster could get injured falling into the bucket. So pile

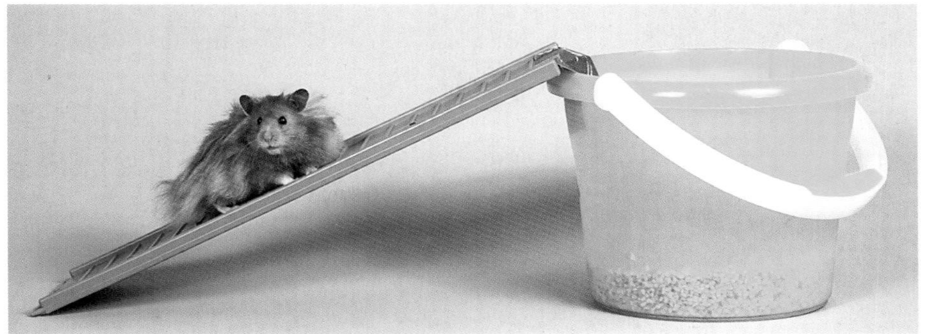

Up the ramp . . .

up lots of cushy bedding for a soft landing. (P.S. The seed bait needs to go on top of the bedding, not on the bottom of the bucket.)

So much for the drop-in-the-bucket approach. Now, are there any other ways to recapture a truant hamster? You could buy or rent a small live-animal trap. Don't be put off by the word *trap* . . . these con-*trap*-tions won't maim or hurt your hamster. They're designed to catch an animal alive and keep it alive until you spring it free. How do they work? You place food, water, and some used sleep house bedding inside. Sooner or later, the hungry and thirsty runaway smells the bait, heads in to investigate, and SLAM goes the door.

Of course, foiling an escape is better than dealing with one—an ounce of prevention will save you mega-headaches. So check that hamster cage and equipment weekly for signs of wear and tear. Tape or lock down the lids of all cage add-ons. *Always* close the cage doors tightly. And *always* keep the door to the hamster's room closed. This way, if she does escape, she'll be confined to one room.

. . . and into the bucket.

Chapter Fifteen

Making the Grade

"A" for effort

Well done! You've worked hard at training, and now you and your hamster have made the grade. Thanks to your patience and perseverance, Tazz has learned to come when called, to use a potty, and to wander on a leash. With your help, his brain is being challenged by a variety of entertaining toys, and it's being stimulated by regular out-of-the-cage playtime. He's getting down to daily fitness training, too, because you've turned his cage into an exercise center with running wheel, ladders, gym bars, and tunnels.

Hamsters are usually solitary souls, but Tazz has learned the social skills he needs to be a great family pet. Most importantly, he has learned to take a relaxed approach to life with humans . . . he is HAPPY.

Learning for the long haul

Now that you've gone to all the trouble of training your hamster, don't slack off. You need to keep up the good work if Tazz is to keep on his toes. Too many hamster owners pay little attention to their pets after the initial novelty wears off. Don't let this happen in your house. For Tazz to stay happy and healthy, he needs your wholehearted commitment, day after day after day.

The more you know about me, the better.

Useful Addresses and Literature

Books

Dwarf Hamsters—A Complete Pet Owner's Manual
Sharon L. Vanderlip
Barron's Educational Series, Inc., 1999

Guide to Owning a Hamster
Anmarie Barrie
T.F.H. Publications, Inc., 1996

Hamsters, A Complete Pet Owner's Manual
Otto Von Frisch
Barron's Educational Series, Inc., 1998

Hamsters: Family Pet Series
Peter Hollmann
Barron's Educational Series, Inc., 1999

Hamsters Today
Dennis Kelsey-Wood
T.F.H. Publications, Inc., 1996

My Hamster and Me
Peter Hollmann
Barron's Educational Series, Inc., 2001

Pet Owner's Guide to the Hamster
Lorraine Hill
Ringpress Books, 1998

The Hamster: An Owner's Guide to a Happy, Healthy Pet
Betsy Sikora Siino
Hungry Minds, Inc., 1997

The Really Useful Hamster Guide
Lorraine Hill
Kingdom Books, 1999

Need some hamster information to chew on? Check books, magazines, and Web sites.

Magazines

Critters USA
P.O. Box 6050
Mission Viejo, CA 92690

Clubs

The American Hamster Association

The British Hamster Association

In order to find these and other hamster clubs, do a Web search on an Internet search engine. Mailing and Web site addresses change frequently.

Index